KidStress

Effective Strategies Parents Can Teach
Their Kids for School, Family, Peers,
the World—and Everything

Georgia Witkin, Ph.D.

KidStress

WHAT IT IS,

HOW IT FEELS,

HOW TO HELP

Viking

VIKING
Published by the Penguin Group
Penguin Putnam Inc., 375 Hudson Street,
New York, New York 10014, U.S.A.
Penguin Books Ltd, 27 Wrights Lane, London W8 5TZ, England
Penguin Books Australia Ltd, Ringwood, Victoria, Australia
Penguin Books Canada Ltd, 10 Alcorn Avenue,
Toronto, Ontario, Canada M4V 3B2
Penguin Books (N.Z.) Ltd, 182–190 Wairau Road,
Auckland 10, New Zealand
Penguin India, 210 Chiranjiv Tower, 43 Nehru Place,
New Delhi 11009, India

Penguin Books Ltd, Registered Offices:
Harmondsworth, Middlesex, England

First published in 1999 by Viking Penguin,
a member of Penguin Putnam Inc.

1   3   5   7   9   10   8   6   4   2

A NOTE TO THE READER

The ideas, procedures, and suggestions contained in this book are not intended as a substitute for medical treatment by a physician. The reader should regularly consult a physician in matters relating to health and particularly with respect to any symptoms that may require diagnosis or medical attention.

LIBRARY OF CONGRESS CATALOGING-IN-PUBLICATION DATA
Witkin, Georgia.
KidStress : what it is, how it feels, how to help / by Georgia Witkin.
p.   cm.
ISBN 0–670–87329–2
1. Stress in children.   2. Stress management for children.   3. Child rearing.
I. Title.   II. Title: KidStress
BF723.S75W58   1999
155.4'18—dc21   98-35457

Printed in the United States of America
Set in Goudy
DESIGNED BY BETTY LEW

To my fabulous "kid," Kimberly,

on the eve of her wedding . . .

with all my love!

Acknowledgments

This book belongs as much to the hundreds of children who took the KidStress Survey as it does to me. They wrote about their worries and fears and fantasies, and their words fill and inspire the pages that follow. They taught me much about childhood stresses, and reminded me how much I'd forgotten about childhood myself.

This book also belongs to my colleagues at The Stress Program at Mt. Sinai Medical Center in New York City, for all their efforts.

To Mt. Sinai Vice President Dr. Gary Rosenberg, for all his encouragement and support.

To my friend and representative Marcy Posner at the William Morris Agency, for her loyalty.

To Mindy Werner and Janet Goldstein at Viking, for being so enthusiastic.

To Perry Garfinkel, for his suggestions, questions, ideas, and editing skills.

To June Goldner and Prodigy, for their creativity and support.

To Judge Milton Mollen, for his words and wisdom.

To my fabulous family: Roy, Carrie, Nikki, Scott, Josh, Jenny, Milton, Carol, Connie, Robert, Chuck, and Mary.

To my darling daughter Kimberly and my new son Travis.

And, as always, to my mother, Dr. Mildred Witkin, for being so smart!

Contents

KidStress

our Children under Stress

An Introduction

Parents love to think of childhood as safe and stress-free. We picture boys and girls playing without a care in the world or securely tucked into bed. We envision them snug as a bug in a rug, as the saying goes.

Maybe it was like that when you grew up. But it's not like that anymore. Childhood these days is highly stressful, as I found in the KidStress Survey undertaken for this book. The survey directly asked children themselves to talk about what stresses them. No previous study, survey, or analysis examining childhood stress had gone to the most knowledgeable and obvious experts in the field—children themselves. But the study on which this book is based did just that.

I took advantage of the new computer technology and, thanks to the support of Prodigy Online, surveyed some eight hundred youngsters between the ages of nine and twelve about their stress. I also surveyed their parents and compared the responses.

Some of the differences between what parents thought their children would say and what the children actually said are breathtaking, surprising, shocking—but they are always enlightening and informative. We must make ourselves aware of such differences or we'll be addressing the wrong problems, and not noticing those we should be addressing. We will be feeling guilty about things that are irrelevant or even untrue. We'll be missing opportunities to help our children help themselves.

Some of kids' stress, of course, comes from the demands of our high-tech, high-impact lifestyles, which are forcing children to cope with real stresses at younger and younger ages—stresses that may not have even existed when we were young. For example:

- Family life is changing. By the year 2000, more than 50 percent of American children will probably live in a single-parent household at some point. There will be more blended families (stepparents, step siblings) than intact families (two biological parents living together).
- More than two million children between the ages of five and thirteen are latchkey kids (kids who are home alone for some time after school).
- Exposure to violence has increased. Children today see more than thirty dead bodies a week on television news programs, thousands more in movies, and an average of thirty acts of violence in cartoons in a given half hour. By the age of twelve, the average child has been witness to more than one hundred thousand hours of violence on TV. The significance of this exposure should not be minimized. According to a Stanford University study of more than one thousand schoolchildren, seeing real-life violence on television news programs may have just as powerful

an effect on young children as experiencing an actual terrifying incident themselves. In fact, in one national survey of seven- to ten-year-olds, 71 percent said they were afraid of getting shot or stabbed at school or at home, and 63 percent worried they might die young.

We also live in an age when more is more, so success- and achievement-oriented parents put pressure on their children to "make it." They push their children to become overachievers. These are the parents who cram their kid's schedule with ballet classes, fencing lessons, soccer practice, and Spanish tutorials (whether the kid wants these lessons or not) because they will look good on the résumé that will get that child into the top schools and the best jobs.

And the world itself is in trouble. Think of all the stresses now we didn't have to think about when we were kids—the deadly disease of AIDS, drive-by shootings, environmental pollution, global warming—the list goes on. All of these create a stress-filled world for youngsters.

But these are not always the stresses children themselves fall asleep worrying about. Their moment-to-moment concerns are quite different. Their own world will fill the pages that follow. "Hearing" their words is vital because "kidstress" can be as damaging as adult stress:

- One in three children suffers from chronic stress symptoms, according to a study conducted in the San Francisco Bay Area.
- Doctors throughout the country are seeing more and more children as young as three years old with stress-related ailments like ulcerative colitis. Studies show that at least one in twenty children under age ten suffers from depression, a typical stress-related condition.

- Suicide is now the third most common form of death among teenagers; eighty thousand will probably attempt it next year.
- Teen pregnancy, often a young person's attempt to escape her own childhood, has increased by 27 percent among younger teens in the last few years, despite a decade of birth-control education. Half a million young women now have children they'll keep, and there's a 30 percent chance they'll get pregnant again within a year.
- Abuse of drugs and alcohol abuse—stress "remedies" that youngsters often see their parents opt for—continues to be on the rise. In fact, in 1997 childhood marijuana use increased for the first time since the government started keeping records.
- Cigarette smoking, another crutch kids often see their parents lean on in times of stress, is now a pediatric disease. Some three thousand youngsters start smoking *every day*.

These are all indicators of two things: one, that our children are suffering from stress; and two, that they are not using the best methods they could to cope with that stress.

WHY ME, WHY NOW?

I come to the investigation of children and stress wearing at least two hats. One, of course, is that of a parent. My daughter is now a lawyer; in fact, she got married as I was finishing this book. Bringing her up was a daily education for me. Watching her grow into a woman of whom I am deeply proud has been a constant joy. Soon, I hope, she will be a mother herself. But as I look back at her childhood, I realize that the world has changed a great deal. If my daughter's world was stressful, her children's world will be even more so.

The other hat is that of a researcher whose career has focused on stress. As assistant clinical professor of psychiatry, director of The Stress Program at Mt. Sinai School of Medicine in New York City, and author of several books on stress (especially *The Female Stress Syndrome*), I have conducted surveys and interviews, sifted through all the latest studies in the field, and listened to and read literally thousands of personal stories about the effects of stress on people's lives.

Most enlightening for me—as a parent and a professional— has been to see that the number one stressor for women has consistently been their concern for their children. My research and the research of others has found that when your child is stressed—is ill, has school or social problems—your life is disrupted. You yourself show the physical and emotional symptoms of stress. You're up all night. You worry. You get sick. Your work suffers. And the stress affects your relationships with those around you: your mate, your other children, your parents and close friends, even your professional colleagues.

When something does stress their children, mothers very often are the ones in charge of "fixing it." They may react by questioning themselves: "What did I do wrong?" "What did I do to cause this?" "Shouldn't I have anticipated this?" "What can I do to make it go away?"

We have these responses because we care. That's what caretaking means, right? Although many fathers are primary caretakers, it is more usually a mother who is in this role. We were brought up for this role; we enjoy the fruits that come from the labor of caretaking, and it upsets us to feel helpless in reducing our child's suffering from stress. And the sense of powerlessness only adds to our stress level.

As I studied the problem of women's stress, it became obvious to me that if my goal was to help women who are mothers help themselves, I had to address childhood stress. I had to help mothers understand what stresses their children and to what degree those stressors are not caused by them. And I had to offer some guidelines for helping parents, mothers in particular, help their children help themselves. And that's what this book is about.

There was another reason my interest grew in investigating childhood stress. As a health contributor for New York's WNBC-TV and now host of "Beyond the News" for Fox News Channel, I am frequently struck by how often the most interesting story in the news is based on new data that absolutely flies in the face of long- and dearly held assumptions, whether those assumptions are about people's health, their expectations of men and women, their values and behaviors—or child rearing.

In terms of audience response, one of the most startling stories I recall is one I reported on shyness. It turns out that shyness is not usually a "psychological affliction" created by overdemanding parents or insecure children but an innate predisposition measurable within weeks of a child's birth. I got many calls from relieved parents who had worried until then that they had been overprotective, overcritical, over . . . parental. I also got calls from adults who had been labeled shy and had suffered their whole lives thinking there was something gravely wrong with them. The same thing happened when I reported that new research shows "only children" are not disadvantaged; in fact, only children have a higher incidence of being more popular and more successful than children with siblings. People stopped me in the street to say they had carried the burden of the "only-child syndrome" for years; now they felt freed of the "syndrome."

What was going on here? I realized we were living our lives—and raising our children—according to myths, half-truths, misconceptions, and incorrect assumptions that needed to be closely reexamined. We needed to take a long, hard look at stereotypes, both positive and negative, and separate fact from fiction. For the children's sake. For our own sake.

This is particularly true when it comes to stress. So I decided to test assumptions about kids and stress in much the same way I investigated the female stress syndrome in the early 1980s. I had asked women firsthand about the stressors in their lives. It was the first comprehensive national survey of women and stress, and I based my conclusions on women's own experiences rather than on doctors' theories, psychological data, or other thirdhand reportage. Now the the KidStress Survey asks *children* firsthand about their stresses.

This type of survey seems to have never before been done, for a few reasons. Until recently there was an assumption that children were pretty naive in their attitudes about themselves and the world around them. "Kids just don't understand how things work" was a typical adult comment, even among my professional colleagues. What I found—and what is corroborated by this research—is that though children may not always have words to express what they're feeling, they're feeling a lot more than we ever thought they were—and much earlier in their lives than we give them credit for. Children do often know what's stressing them, whether they used the word "stress" or not.

Another reason this type of survey hadn't been done was that until now we did not have the technology to poll children directly, nor could we poll them anonymously so they could feel free to answer honestly without fear of incrimination. With increasingly greater numbers each year, kids are now on-line at home and at school. So with the assistance of Prodigy, I designed a questionnaire for children on one Web site and on a different site I asked parents to tell us how they thought children would respond. Those parents' responses became our "instrument of prediction," as psychologists call it. (You can read the surveys in the appendix—and feel free to take them yourself.)

We also administered the survey to children who were not on-line in order to corroborate that children using computers were not a specialized group and, with very few exceptions, the patterns were the same.

HOW THIS BOOK IS ORGANIZED AND HOW TO USE IT

If you are eager to find out exactly what children say stresses them, you can jump ahead to chapter 2, in which I report on the key findings that separate what parents believe from what children report. But first let's talk about how I've organized this book, why I've done it this way, and how you can use it as a guide.

In chapter 2, as I just said, you will read the children's responses to the stress poll; these form the foundation of this book. In chapter 3, I explain the basics of stress: how it becomes triggered and which physical, emotional, and behavioral signs can tell you that your child is suffering from it, even when your child can't find the grown-up words for it.

Chapters 4 through 9 follow up on each of the major areas of stress that children told us about. In these chapters, you'll hear in great detail what children say and feel, and read suggestions for helping children deal with the symptoms of stress.

In chapter 10 we take a closer look at the typical day-to-day situations in a child's world that cause stress, along with suggestions for solutions.

But even more than specific suggestions for alleviating your child's stress, throughout all these chapters you will find again and again two basic overriding principles that are meant to serve as your guide:

- First, realize that children will have stress—sometimes significant amounts of it—in their lives. It's natural. It's normal. Therefore, we parents should not deny it, not say, "You have nothing to be stressed out about." Nor can we chastise ourselves for the stress our children may feel, because feeling stressed at times is part of being human. We parents cannot "make it go away."

- Second, don't assume that what stresses you will stress your child, or that the coping strategy you use to alleviate your stress will work for your youngster. We are all "programmed," if you will, differently, and adults really are different from children when it comes to stress.

What you *can* do is begin to recognize the signs that indicate our children are feeling stress, the mostly physical or behavioral but sometimes verbal messages they try to send to let us know they are overwhelmed by a stressful situation. Each child may use her own "lyrics" to communicate this to you, but the "melody" will be the same.

- Notice what your child does *naturally* to try to cope with stress. This is important: children have their own built-in stress management systems in addition to their own individual capabilities. Some kids use their imagination to escape from chaos; some use "pretend" to practice for a scary future. Some get active to burn up anger or anxiety; some get quiet to digest bad news. Some are soothed by music or movement or their mothers; some seem to sleep it off or talk a blue streak.

- With humor, with sympathy, with simple logic, with perspective, help get the dilemma down to *child size*—by that I mean reduce it from an overwhelming predicament to a task that can be handled—and you will teach your child two invaluable lessons. First, that while some people, things, or events cause him (and many of us) stress, there are ways to reduce the effect of that stress on his body and his mind. And second, that he doesn't always need you to solve all his stress problems.

One more thing you can do to help your child deal better with stress is to be a role model. As is so often the case in parenting, how you yourself deal with situations serves as a blueprint that your kids can follow. Don't try to hide the fact that sometimes you too feel stress. Not feeling and reacting to stress would be abnormal. Instead, show your kids that you know how to deal with it. Let them know that the deadline pressure at work is why you have a headache, then let them know that taking an invigorating walk around the neighborhood is how you make the headache go away. It doesn't make the cause of the headache go away—that deadline is still there—but it does put you in a much better frame of mind to deal with that deadline. Your children will, hopefully, watch you go through the transformation from being a stressed-out and impatient parent to being a more mellow person, and they will infer that, yes, stress is part of life and that, yes, there are easily accessible built-in tools to help them deal.

Now it's time to listen to the children. Their words and the revelations you'll read about in this book will cast your own children in a new light. Use this book to enter into their world, to learn their secret language of stress, to unearth clues that explain their behavior, and ultimately to empower them to take greater control of their own lives.

CHAPTER 2

Children (and Parents) Report What Stresses Them

The Results of the KidStress Survey

Are your children under stress? Do you know how much stress they're under? Do you know what stresses them? Do you know the symptoms? Do you know how much of their stress is due to your influence? How much comes from peer pressure? School pressure? Do you know what they can do to help themselves deal with their stress? Do you know what you can do to help them deal with it?

You may think you know the answers to these questions. After all, nobody knows your kids like you do. Not only that, but you used to be a child and now you read all those magazine and newspaper articles and listen to reports on TV about stress. But what do we adults really know about children's stress? Not as much as we think!

- Parents underestimate how much children worry.
- Parents underestimate how alone many children feel.

- Parents underestimate how much insomnia children have when they are stressed.
- Parents underestimate how often children are afraid to talk to them.
- Parents underestimate school stress and overestimate peer pressure.
- Parents underestimate how often children's fears are realistic.
- Parents underestimate how much of children's sadness is altruistic.

How do I know all this? The KidStress Survey!

One thing I found in the survey was a wide gap between the myths and the realities of kidstress. Even as a parent myself, I was amazed by much of what children told us about their stressors. Let's first look at what parents *think* stresses their children. To bring home the discrepancy between our assumptions and children's realities, I encourage you to complete the parents' survey before you read on. You'll find it on page 200. Then compare your answers to those of the other parents. The survey found most parents *believe*

- That their children worry, but not "a lot."
- That their children's greatest source of stress is peer pressure.
- That doing well at school is less important to children than being popular or liked.
- That the fear of being punished is less important to children than being popular or liked.
- That children do not worry about their parents' health.
- That stomachaches are the most frequent physical stress symptom for children and headaches rank number two.

- That fighting with a sibling is the most frequent behavioral stress symptom and crying is number two.
- That they give their children some say about what they do.
- That their children are not usually afraid to tell or ask them anything.

By the way, as mentioned earlier, the answers and predictions given by a control group of parents who were not on-line were very similar to those given by the computer-polled parents, but they varied in one instance: the computer-based parents predicted that children's greatest source of stress would be peer pressure, but the control group of parents predicted that children would be more worried about doing well in school, failing, or trying something new. The control group was closer to the truth. Perhaps families who don't use home computers talk to each other more.

If you have compared these results to your own answers and found them to be similar, you probably share most parents' point of view about children's stress. We assume that the most frequent physical symptoms of stress are those we hear about the most (stomachaches and headaches) and that the most frequent behavioral symptoms are those we see the most (fighting or crying). We assume that children's greatest concerns have to do with peer pressure, not school or our well-being, because children usually talk about their friends and their changing social worlds, not about school or our well-being. We assume that our children feel some sense of control over their daily lives, and feel free to confide in us, because we'd like them to feel that way.

All understandable. All well meaning. All seemingly well informed.

All wrong.

WHAT CHILDREN TOLD US

According to the children who took the survey, childhood is not carefree. It can't be, because *all change is stressful* (even good change) and young people's lives are filled with change. (I will explain in greater detail the physical, behavioral, and emotional components of stress in chapter 3.) Here are just some of the changes children reported to us in the survey:

- 72 percent say they've had a pet die.
- 51 percent have changed schools at least once.
- 45 percent have also moved to a new town or city.
- 45 percent experienced the birth of a brother or sister.
- 35 percent say they are aware of family money troubles.
- 20 percent have parents who are divorced.
- 18 percent have at least one parent who has been severely ill.
- 12 percent are dealing with a parent's second spouse.

Children themselves, of course, don't speak about "change," but their answers to the survey questions tell us they have some worries we don't suspect. What follows is a complete report of children's answers. Compare them to your children's answers, and to your own.

Question 1: Do You Ever Worry?

	Children's Answers	*Parents' Predictions*
A lot	31%	21%
Sometimes	53	59

Not often	12	15
Not at all	2	3

NOTE: Totals don't always equal 100 percent since numbers are rounded off.

Children answered this question with a resounding yes. In fact, a combined total of only 14 percent of the children surveyed said "not often" or "not at all." *The rest, almost 85 percent, said they certainly do worry,* and 31 percent said they worry a lot.

Only 21 percent of parents predicted that children would say they worry a lot. Most parents thought the majority of children would say they worry sometimes, and they were generally correct. But almost one in three children say they worry more than sometimes, and those numbers are 10 percent higher than parents had guessed.

Question 2: If You Do Worry, What Kind of Things Do Concern You?

Remember, parents predicted that children would be most worried about their friends not liking them and kids making fun of them—in other words, peer pressure. However, when we looked at the answers children gave, we found that peer pressure does *not* lead their list. The following is how children ranked what stresses them.

1. School Stresses. Parents may be surprised, even delighted, to know that school concerns lead the list! Grades are the greatest worry among those children who say that school causes stress; then come tests, homework, and passing.

2. Family Worries. Now, here's another surprise for parents. Peer pressures and peer concerns are not even second on the children's stress list. Worrying about family and parents' health ranks second. These worries probably aren't realistic in most cases. Children haven't lived long enough to have a deep perspective on their parents' well-being. Nor is it a protective love. Children are too much in need of protection themselves to be giving out protection. Their worries, I suspect, probably come from children's self-protective impulses. They want us to be well so that we can keep them well.

3. Peer Pressures. The bullies, the gangs, the fickle friends, the teasing, the informal initiations, the codes of conduct—parents may have thought peer pressure would lead the children's stress list because their own memories of these stresses are so vivid. But we grew up in an era of the extended family and less nightly news; our major concern may have been as innocent as whether we were accepted by our friends. Today's children may not have that luxury. But this doesn't mean that peer pressure doesn't exist. In fact, the percentage for this concern was almost the same as that for family worries.

4. The World. Are children stressed by news reports about pollution, global warming, viral pandemics, and flesh-eating bacteria? By action films about terrorist bombings, nuclear accidents, and germ warfare? By warnings about ticks on their pets, kiddie porn and seducers on the Internet, and even sunshine in the schoolyard? (Did you know that many pediatricians now recommend that children wear sunscreen every day?) Do they actively think about these problems, or is all this just background noise to them?

Children worry about the world more than parents think they do—much more. Only about 10 percent of parents predicted their children would say they were stressed by pollution and war concerns; about 40 percent predicted crime would worry their children more. The truth, according to our survey, is that children worry about safe water and air and nuclear war almost four times more than they worry about crime!

5. The Future and Everything. Next are two categories of children's stress that parents didn't anticipate: fears about the future and fears about "everything," as one respondent succinctly put it. Even though a year is still a vague concept to children under eight years of age, and ten years seems like an eternity to a twelve-year-old who smokes and drinks, the future is still scary to many of them (22 percent). Besides, many of their future fears are really current worries and concerns too overwhelming for them to deal with; in other words, their present forces them to think about their future.

Then there are the children who deal with current stress not by projecting it into the future but by generalizing it. Instead of listing specific problems, they say everything stresses them (16 percent). It's less embarrassing, they reason, to be stressed by everything than by homework or parents. It also stops any real discussion of the stress.

6. Missing Stresses. Perhaps the biggest surprise for parents is what's *missing* from the children's list of stressors: fears of being punished, being hurt, or getting sick. Almost 45 percent of parents said they thought children are concerned about being punished, 28 percent of parents thought children are stressed by fear of being hurt, and 15 percent thought children are worried about getting sick. However, there were few references to any of these on the children's lists. Children may feel far more invincible than parents think!

7. What, Me Worry? An interesting footnote: a few parents (3 percent) predicted that children would say they don't worry about anything. Whether this prediction came from optimism,

fond childhood memories of their own, naïveté, wishful thinking, or condescension, it was wrong. *Not one child* gave that answer in their own words. Even though 2 percent checked off
"not at all" to the question "Do you ever worry?" when it came
time to fill in the blank for question 2, every child named at
least one stressor.

Question 3: When You Get Worried or Nervous, Do You Ever Have Any Physical Reactions?

Without the words to express their stress, children often express it with their bodies. When a child is overwhelmed, his
head will hurt with the effort to organize his thoughts. If a
situation is gut-wrenching, his gut or stomach may literally react. If life has become a nightmare, nightmares may be the
stress symptom.

Here's a comparison of the physical stress symptoms that
parents notice and the physical symptoms that children say
they feel:

Symptom	*% Children Reporting*	*% Parents Predicting*
Insomnia	47%	35%
Stomachaches	44	52
Feel sick	26	24
Headaches	21	40
Jumpy	9	32
Sweaty	4	14

Parents are clearly aware that stomachaches, headaches, insomnia, and feeling sick can all mean a child is under stress. In
fact, except for insomnia, parents may be overdiagnosing some
of these symptoms. Meanwhile, children add the following
stress-related symptoms that some parents miss:

- Butterflies or knots in the stomach
- Rapid heartbeat
- Feeling very tired
- Dizziness
- Light-headedness
- Feeling shaky
- Nausea
- Vomiting
- Sweaty palms
- Shaky hands or knees

Question 7: Do You Do Any of the Following?

Behavior	% Children Reporting	% Parents Reporting
Withdraw (want to be alone)	65%*	35%
Fight with siblings	60	54
Daydream a lot	51*	26
Bite nails	50	42
Have trouble sleeping	47*	35
Cry easily	43	48
Trouble concentrating (trouble with homework)	41	40
Get distracted in school	30	33
Feel sick a lot	26	24
Suck thumbs	9	14

*Invisible symptom

Although parents do seem to have a handle on their children's observable stress behaviors, like crying easily, nail biting, school problems, sibling rivalry, and feeling sick, they don't seem to be aware of the toll stress takes in ways that can't be seen—the invisible symptoms. The starred items in the table above tell the story of the secret symptoms.

"Thinking," however, is as much a behavior as running or jumping or talking, and as easily affected by stress. Unlike physical behaviors, though, we can't see stressful thinking; it's not always obvious even to the astute naked eye. Children's responses to the survey tell us more about the prevalence of their secret symptoms:

- The majority of the children say they want to be alone when they're worried or scared, but only one in three parents knows it or thinks it's true.
- Fifty percent of all the children say they daydream a lot when they are stressed, but only 25 percent of parents know that or think it's true.
- Almost 50 percent of the children say they have trouble sleeping when they are stressed, but only 35 percent of the parents guessed that was so.

What we see is apparently not always what we get. We may think we see sullenness or shyness when in reality children are withdrawing due to stress. We may think we see lack of motivation or learning disabilities when children are actually escaping stress by daydreaming. We may think we're seeing a spoiled child who won't go to sleep or an insecure one who calls out to us all night long when she's probably suffering from insomnia or nightmares, two warnings signs of stress.

Question 4: Do You Ever Have Nightmares?
Nightmares top the list of children's stress symptoms. Parents

say they notice their children's stomachaches most often, followed by their headaches, but more than 65 percent of the kids said they have nightmares at least once in a while, and another 8 percent said they have nightmares a lot. That's almost 75 percent of children reporting nightmares at least sometimes, while only 37 percent of the parents say they know it. So why are parents missing the signs? Certainly not for lack of concern. It's more likely a matter of timing. That is, nightmares are most likely to occur in the early-morning hours when parents are often busy or unavailable. Children are often able to handle the bad dream themselves because when they wake up their room is light and they're distracted by the start of the day's activities. (For more on nightmares and insomnia, see chapter 8.)

Question 5: How Much Say Do You Have about What You Do?

Children were given the following answer choices for this question:

1. I can choose.
2. I have some say.
3. I don't have much say.
4. I have no say about these things.

Almost 30 percent of the children said they can choose. That means about one in three thinks he is in control of such things as when he goes to bed, what he eats, and how he spends his day. But the vast majority of parents don't agree. Seventy-five percent of the parents polled on-line said their children may have some say but not free choice; 89 percent of parents taking the non-computer-based control survey said the same thing.

Do these children say they feel in charge of their daily life because their parents are so skilled at directing them that the children don't feel controlled? A nice idea, but unlikely since there are still many unsavory things children tell us they have to do, like "clean the pet cage," "get up at 7:30 A.M.," "do chores," and "take tests."

The reason so many children think they are in charge of their daily life is more likely that so many parents aren't around after school. These are not necessarily delinquent parents, just busy parents who work long hours to support the family. That's no excuse, you may be thinking; our great-grandparents were just as busy. Yes, but back then, sociologists and historians tell us, many children also worked in the family business or did chores and repairs around the house. When they did play, it was usually under the supervision of an extended family or community of neighbors. Everyone knew each other and was in each other's business. They also knew each other's children. Less unstructured time and more adult presence probably served children well since having choices within a routine or schedule is ideal for children. Some strategies for how to do this in today's world are discussed in chapter 10.

Question 6: Are You Ever Afraid to Tell or Ask Your Parents Anything?

Response	Children	Parents
Sometimes	48%	50%
Rarely	28	37
All the time	15	3
Never	9	9

Children use expressions like "Your mom's gonna kill you when she finds out" or "You're finished if your dad hears about this," but does this mean that children are really afraid of their parents? Some are. Many should be. A University of New Hampshire study found that 63 percent of American children are victims of a parent's verbal aggression, and the U.S. Department of Justice estimates that 2.8 million children in the United States are abused or neglected—and that as many as one-third of child abuse cases may go undetected or unreported. Also frightening, child abuse crosses all boundaries of age, race, and social class. (For more information, write to the National Child Abuse and Neglect Data System in Washington, D.C., and ask for the "Child Abuse and Neglect Fact Sheet, National Clearinghouse on Child Abuse and Neglect Information.")

But this question was not designed to reveal abuse. It was directed at the stress a child may feel when, in the normal course of daily living, she must ask or tell her parents something upsetting. The answers suggest a sad and frightening story. Although only 3 percent of parents predicted that their children would say they are afraid to tell or ask parents anything all the time, an incredible 15 percent of kids did say that. I read such comments as "My stepdad yells," "My dad hurts me," "I make my parents angry," and "My parent is drunk."

Meanwhile, surprisingly few children and parents said communications were always open, despite experts' constant reminders that encouraging children to feel that they can talk to their parents about anything can help lower the risk of drug use, involvement in gangs or cults, or unsafe sexual behavior. Fewer than one in ten children said they feel that there is open communication with their folks. Fewer than one in ten parents expect more.

Question 9 (We asked children to complete a series of sentences. Here are the results and what they may suggest.)
If children were telling their parents everything, what would we be hearing? The KidStress Survey may be our first opportunity to find out. On-line and anonymous, children completed many open-ended questions about their private feelings. They

wrote about what makes them mad and sad, what makes them scared, what turns them off and on about having a sibling, and what they wish they didn't have to do. First, their anger.

"I get angry when . . ."

Children said they get angry about the following, in this order:

- Inequality, injustice, and human cruelty
- Siblings' behaviors
- Disloyal and hurtful friends
- Dictatorial parents

When children spoke of anger at their parents, it was primarily for yelling or being dictatorial when children felt such behavior was overreaction. Two examples of how they finished the sentence "I get angry when . . .":

> "my dad starts yelling and stuff for no reason."
> "my mom gets mad and takes everything out on me
>   when it is not all my fault."

Even more children were angry at siblings, mainly for bugging them, fighting with them, being mean, and taking their things—in that order (by the way, brothers got more complaints than sisters). They wrote:

> "my brother hits me."
> "my brother goes into my room without permission."
> "my sister tells on me or if I get a bad grade."

Many children say they are angry at the behavior of friends and other children, and acts of disloyalty led the list. For example:

"kids insult me about my height."
"I get in trouble, picked on, bullied, left out of things,
    made fun of, and teased."

One of the biggest surprises of the survey results, however, was that most of the children focused the majority of their anger on inequities, injustice, and human cruelty or weakness—not on personal or petty complaints. These responses tell us that our children certainly absorb headlines and newscasts, certainly hear and see all that is happening around them, and certainly care very much. Anger about insensitivity and judgmental attitudes leads their list:

"people make fun of other or elderly people."
"people let fear and hate govern the way they and others
    live."
"people judge people on appearance."

More than any other generation that has ever lived, our children are bombarded with images and reports of human disaster—locally, nationally, internationally. We can supervise what they watch on television, choose which magazines and newspapers come into the house, and discuss all news stories that may be upsetting them. But we must do more than that, I believe. We must find the good in our lives, and the good behind the news stories to talk about, too. For instance, we can

- Point out the bravery of firefighters and rescue
  workers.
- Note the generosity of communities that help out
  families of murder victims.
- Explain the work of public defenders (and avoid the
  lawyer jokes).

- Find exciting science, medical, and technological news stories to keep them interested in the future.
- Do local charity work as a family so they can make use of their anger in the present.

Remind your children that feeling *helpless* about the things that make us angry is more destructive and stressful than just feeling angry. Help them help others and you'll be helping children help themselves.

"I get sad when . . ."

This survey item revealed another surprise: the sources of children's sadness. Parents predicted that children would be most upset about friends not liking them, other children making fun of them, being punished, or failing at something. The answers children gave, so very different from those predictions, force us to rethink some basic assumptions about children's emotions. The children surveyed were less saddened by personal and social setbacks than by the loss of loved ones and the pain of others. In other words, the same kinds of events and losses that upset adults also sadden children. The children's survey responses are all the more poignant when you keep in mind that the majority of those polled were nine to twelve years old, the balance even younger.

Death saddens children the most, according to the poll, especially the death of a loved one or a pet. Their sadness is not superficial; children are quite seriously feeling the loss and carrying the sadness that death brings. It would be wrong to refute or belittle, to brush off or in any way discredit this real emotional sadness with, say, a reassuring platitude like "Grandma is in heaven now." Once children reach eight or nine years of age, they are not likely to forget the deceased. In chapter 9, I'll discuss how we can help them deal with the stress that comes with the loss of a loved one.

Loss is also the theme of the second most frequent response. Children are saddened, they say, when someone they care about moves away or leaves them. Here are typical responses to "I feel sad when . . .":

"my sister goes away to her school."
"my parents go away on trips without me."
"a friend is moving."

The next most frequent cause for children's sadness is not peer problems, as parents had predicted. It's parent problems. Children tell us they are saddened and stressed when their parents fight frequently or seem upset with each other. Completing the sentence "I get sad when . . ." were these statements:

"my dad gets mad for some reason."
"my mom and stepdad fight."
"I think about my parents being separated and divorced."

They are saddened or stressed when their parents look "mean in their eyes," as one child said. And when . . .

"my mom ignores me so she can spend time with her new husband."
"my parents say they're going to sell my dog for no reason at all."
"my dad hits my cats for fun."

They are also sad when they think their parents are sad, that is, when . . .

"I let my mom down."
"my dad looks depressed."

And they are equally concerned about the rest of their family, that is, when . . .

> "people make fun of my little sister because she has apraxia."
> "I think about my grandma, who is sick."

This capacity for empathy is even more obvious when the children are *not* talking about parents or other family members. Their sadness and concern often extend far beyond their own immediate problems, far beyond what we expect from children so young. For example, "I get sad when . . .":

> "people hurt others."
> "bad things happen to innocent people."
> "I see homeless kids, and when animals are sick."

Even when children do refer to very personal reasons for feeling sad, those reasons are rarely trivial, self-centered, or selfish. They are more likely to be thoughtful, and heartbreaking. They said, "I get sad when . . .":

> "I look in a mirror."
> "nobody wants to play with me."
> "people make fun of me."

"I get scared when . . ."

What could be scarier for a child—at least in a parent's mind—than being home alone, being in the dark, seeing a frightening movie, or some other classic terror? Children in the poll tell us that their *parents' behavior* is more scary. Now that's scary! When their parents fight, get angry, or lose control, emotionally or physically, children report the most stress. When . . .

> "my family members fight a lot around me and get
>   very loud."
> "my mom drives drunk."

The second most fearful experience, children tell us, is being alone. Think about the two million children who come home every day after school to an empty house, and the many others who are left alone at night or with baby-sitters not much older than themselves. "I get scared," they wrote, "when . . .":

> "I'm alone in the house and hear noises."
> "I am walking alone at night."
> "I know that one day I must face the world alone."

If your work or other responsibilities demand that you must leave your child or children alone—and nowadays many parents eventually face such a situation—check chapter 10, in which I offer several guidelines and suggestions for helping kids cope with the stress of being alone.

If you're wondering how much effect fright films, terror television, or news shows have on these children, the answer is clear: they have a powerful effect, for two reasons. First, children have an innate fear of loud noises and darkness, the main ingredients of scary shows. Those fears usually don't begin to fade until children are at least seven or eight years old. Actually, that's when they become more afraid of being teased by friends who call them "scaredy cats" than of the movies, so they practice managing and suppressing the fear. The second reason is that although children may know intellectually that a movie or TV show isn't real, they don't know it *emotionally*.

The fictional images are saved in their brain alongside real-life images, and both pop up in the middle of the night when strange noises and shapes need explanation.

Here's what some children themselves said in the poll when asked to finish the sentence "I get scared when . . .":

"I'm by myself at night."
"I watch horror movies with the door or window open."
"Stalkers and killers are on TV channels."

In later chapters, we'll take a closer look at what scares children and how to determine whether they're ready for *Jurassic Park*.

Besides the fear of things that go bump in the night, children's fears are surprisingly realistic. Some kids are afraid of animals, many of natural disasters, some of violence. There was only one mention of aliens in more than one thousand responses. Among the fears based on real-life experiences, children told us, "I get scared when . . .":

"I hear gunshots."
"my dad goes to work, because he is a cop and I'm worried."
"tornado sirens go off."

It's not a parent's job to make *all* these fears go away, especially considering that we couldn't make many of the real-life problems go away even if we wanted to. Besides, having some degree of fear may even help children survive in today's world. But we can make sure that children are not overwhelmed by these fears. Later I'll offer ways to help them develop strategies for "de-stressing."

"My parents get angry at me when . . ."

One reason children may be telling their parents less about their stresses than their parents predicted is because parents themselves are frequently the *source of* the stress. Did you notice in the children's responses that parental anger ranks as one of the most frequent reasons kids give for feeling anger, sadness, and fear? When we asked children why their parents get angry at them, we were surprised to find that they don't think it's because of their dirty rooms and undone chores. Instead, children seem to sense that a lack of respect or a lack of conscience is far more upsetting to parents—which shows that we don't always give kids enough credit for their awareness. When asked anonymously on-line and off-line to complete the sentence "My parents get angry at me when . . ." kids gave these representative responses:

> "I take things."
> "I lie."
> "I disobey."
> "I don't give them respect."
> "I do something bad or yell and be disrespectful."
> "I talk back."
> "I don't try hard enough, when they think that I
>   can do a lot better."
> "I do something really, really bad."
> "I give attitude."
> "I do something that they know that I know
>   was the wrong thing to do."

One area in which children (whether older or younger, boy or girl, surveyed by computer or not) seem to agree is that their parents get angry at them when they fight with their siblings.

Next on the list of things that make their parents angry, say the children, come school, homework, grades, and teacher's reports.

But the sentence repeated (almost word for word) most often by the children is "My parents get angry at me when I don't listen to them." Are they saying they are being negative, rebellious, foolish, distracted, disrespectful, headstrong, independent, passive-aggressive, or just plain disobedient? From child to child, and situation to situation, any or all of the above may apply. But somehow, it appears, both parents and children seem to know exactly what this sentence means.

Finally, we all know that certain rebellious behaviors can be part of the ongoing drama between parent and child, but parents can take at least some solace in knowing how universal these behaviors are. From children who have moved into puberty, when anybody in "authority" becomes the enemy, some of the comments sound almost like defiant boasts, suggesting that kids know exactly what to do to push our buttons. Some examples: "My parents get angry at me when . . .":

"I drink too much."
"I come home late, argue, get in trouble with police, get in
        trouble at school, cuss at teachers, stay at my boyfriend's
        house, sneak out, and lots of other stuff."
"I get a new piercing or hair color or when my grades drop."
"I threaten to kick their ass."
"I refuse to bathe."
"I throw stuff in the house."

"I wish I didn't have to . . ."

Besides asking kids what they think their parents don't want them to do, the poll also asked what they'd prefer not having to do. Although children typically don't make a secret of their answers to this question, it's still informative to see which answers are given most often. In order of frequency, they wish they didn't have to

Go to school and/or do homework.
Do chores (clean their room, make their bed, wash dishes).
Deal with siblings (share a room, baby-sit).

Although the above list accounts for almost 80 percent of the responses, the other 20 percent of the responses let us know how very stressed young children *can* feel, and how frustrating it must be for them to live in a world in which they often feel they do not have control. They said, "I wish I didn't have to . . .":

"go to another funeral."
"live this life anymore."
"watch my mother work every day and struggle. I wish we had money."
"get wrapped up in my parents' fighting."
"be in such a messed-up world filled with greedy humans and dead animals."
"live with racist white bigots."
"choose between one parent and another."
"deal with the violence of kids in my class."
"worry that we will go flat broke and live in a carton box on the street."
"be a Christian kid in an un-Christ-like world."

"The best part of having a brother or sister is . . ."
"The worst part of having a brother or sister is . . ."

Finally, what about those bundles of joy that your first children begged you for—brothers and sisters? You probably thought your children would play together and give each other comfort in later years. You had heard of sibling rivalry, but you were not prepared for its day-to-day manifestations: the finger-pointing, the pinching and pushing, the why-can't-I-if-she-can competitiveness, the sheer torture they inflict on each other. I was astonished to see with what frequency the words "my brother" or "my sister" started children's responses when we asked them to complete the sentence "I get angry when . . ."

To find out more, we asked children what they think is the best part, and the worst part, of having a brother or sister. There was enormous agreement in the answers to both questions. Four times more than any other answer was that the seemingly nonstop fighting is the worst part of having a sibling. A close second is the complaint that their sibs violate their privacy. Another major complaint is that their siblings get them into trouble with their parents. Some kids had more individualized complaints, like feeling that parental attention is divided, having to share their parents' affection, and having to baby-sit.

There is good news too. Though your kids might not tell it to you (and perhaps never will until you are well past retirement), they told it to us. Completing the sentence "The best part of having a brother or sister is . . ." the most frequent answer was "having someone to play with." But children went far beyond seeing their sibling as just a personal companion or convenience. Although a few gave faint praise or made snide remarks—like "having someone to boss around" or "I can pick on them"—many more recognized the important, intrinsic emotional role a sibling can fill, seen in such responses as these:

"having someone around who knows how I feel sometimes."
"they watch out for you, and stick up for you."
"you have a good friend forever."
"I can ask them questions and confide in them what I can't
    with my parents."
"they watch out for you."
"lots of love."

With all that positive stuff going on (even if it's well concealed), siblings can help each other manage stress. It's a delicate art, but it's possible. In chapter 5 I'll add some suggestions for how to encourage that. And for those parents whose children don't have siblings, I'll also share some good news about only children. (Clue: it turns out that they are not socially or emotionally challenged, as our grandparents—and maybe you—had thought.)

THE NEW REALITIES OF RAISING CHILDREN UNDER STRESS

As you can see, when it comes to kidstress, things are not as we had thought. It may be hard for us to let go of beliefs about child rearing that have been passed down from generation to generation, to turn our back on articles we've read or reports we've heard, to discard old tales and parenting folklore that we've accepted as true. It may even be hard to abandon first-hand assumptions we have made about our own children. But to gain the greatest value from this book, that's exactly what I'm asking of you: to suspend your beliefs and be willing to accept a new parenting plan, based on the wisdom of your children.

CHAPTER 3

kids' Bodies, kids' minds, kids' stress

Before we talk about the stresses in their lives, let's first understand how stress affects children's bodies and minds. This chapter is for your information and yours alone. If you try to explain the physical whys and psychological wherefores of stress to your children, it will just go over their heads. They couldn't care less about the ebbs and flows of hormonal changes, the vagaries of the autonomic nervous system, and the other physiological phenomena of stress. Your explanation of these intricacies will have about as much interest to them as a PBS special on the economic aspects of the Spanish-American War. Especially don't try to describe all this when they are in the middle of a stress-induced temper tantrum; you'll probably only make matters worse. Whenever they're stressed, all they want to know is how to make the "bad" feeling go away.

You, however, may be comforted by knowing how the body and the mind work together to trigger the stress syndrome in children. Understanding what causes this syndrome—and why—will help you recognize it and will give you a bit of objectivity. At the very least, knowing that some stress (and your child's reaction to it) is natural will take part of the pressure off you. I will make the same point throughout this book: your child's stress is not always due to something you've done wrong.

THE FIGHT-OR-FLIGHT RESPONSE

Child or adult, male or female, we all are in possession of an inborn life-saving capacity called the fight-or-flight response. Its purpose is to prepare us to deal with and respond to change, any change, whether good or bad. Win the lottery and your heart will probably beat faster. By the same token, slam on your brakes to avoid hitting another car and your heart rate will spike. Put a double scoop of your child's favorite ice cream in front of him and his heart rate will probably jump. Scold him for writing his initials on your living-room wall with a permanent marker and his body will react the same way.

The fight-or-flight response can be triggered by something as subtle as moving into a too-crowded elevator or as obvious as a noise in the night. Our heart beats faster, our eyes dilate, our palms sweat, our cheeks flush. There's a pounding in our chest or in our head.

In the 1930s, the Austrian-born endocrinologist Hans Selye called this effect a "nonspecific response of the body to any demand placed on it," or the general adaptation syndrome. This innate ability is also called the stress response or, as I mentioned, the fight-or-flight response. It's called that because in a much earlier time—when people lived in caves, not condos—this internal mechanism helped us mobilize to deal with predators that crossed our paths. Or it enabled us to deal with the unknowns we encountered in the course of hunting and gathering. And in those days (not unlike these days) both the

predators and the unknowns were many. In the flash of a moment we were left with a choice: to stay and fight that saber-
toothed tiger (or whatever) or to turn tail and run for our lives.
Since either action provoked fright, we suddenly needed all the
physical fortitude and mental acuity we could muster.

Under such pressure, the body's fight-or-flight, plus fright,
system kicks into gear, stimulating the chemical, physical, and
psychological forces within us into a state of preparedness.
These forces ready us to cope with the worst-case scenario: a
life-threatening situation. We are thrust into a three-alarm
state of emergency. Stress! Stress! Stress!

In an instant, our body's nervous and endocrine (hormonal)
systems are activated. Stress signals are sent along three path-
ways of the nervous system. They travel from the brain through
the motor nerves to our arms, legs, and muscles along the skele-
ton. Presumably we're going to need our limbs to fight off the
foe or run for our lives. The stress signals also travel from the
brain to the autonomic nervous system. That raises our blood
pressure, heart rate, and blood-sugar level; it also releases a re-
serve of red blood cells carrying oxygen to muscles. The combination of blood sugar and oxygen helps those muscles to work
at the highest levels of efficiency. These signals also slow our
digestive process, since eating is the last thing that would be
on our mind if we were being chased by a wild beast. Finally,
the stress signals travel from the brain to the interior of the
gland that releases adrenaline, a general stimulant, into the
bloodstream. Again, we're going to need all the extra energy
we can get.

Meanwhile, the stress message also travels *within* the brain
to the hypothalamus, which acts as our emotional center. This
triggers the endocrine, or hormonal, system. This system works
more slowly than the nervous system, but what it lacks in speed
it makes up for in endurance. That's why long after a stressful
experience has ended your heart is still pounding and you are

still worrying about what could have happened or what you should have done.

THE SHORT-TERM AND THE LONG-TERM EFFECTS OF STRESS

There are two kinds of stress: immediate and constant. For example, if you're a kid there's the *immediate* stress of a bully walking toward you, and the *constant* stress of having to face that bully every morning for the rest of the school year.

The problem is that your body is best designed to respond to immediate, short-term stress. If the stress is constant, long-term, and relentless, your body has little time to relax and recover between stress attacks. After all, the heart, which begins to pump harder in response to stress, is just another muscle. Overwork it and it will tire.

The same goes for your respiratory system. When under stress, you breathe more rapidly, often twice as fast as normal. Your breathing becomes more shallow too; you end up panting. In a short-term stressful situation, this is necessary. When this pattern becomes chronic, however, your nose and mouth dry up, and the muscles in your diaphragm may start to hurt from working so hard. If this goes on too long, dizziness and a feeling of always being out of breath may result. This condition, caused by expelling too much carbon dioxide from your lungs, is called hyperventilation, a common symptom of prolonged stress.

Continuous stress can lead to other, longer-term problems too. If your child complains of constant tummy aches, the cause may be more than eating too much junk food. It could be the result of unabated stress. When the stress button keeps getting pushed, the rhythmic smooth-muscle contractions that push food through the intestinal system slow down (responding, as I mentioned earlier, to signals from the autonomic nervous system). Glands that produce the gastric juices used to break down food may also slow down, further diminishing the stomach's ability to digest. Meanwhile, there can be an increase of stomach acid due to other hormonal activity. All this can cause serious gastrointestinal problems by irritating stomach walls. Does this mean children with ulcers?

Probably not. New research has shown that ulcers are not directly caused by stress but by a little bacteria called *Helicobacter pylori,* or *H. pylori.* However, long-term stress may help *H. pylori* do the job by making stomach walls more vulnerable to invasion. And at the very least, stress can cause those tummy aches.

KIDS' STRESS AND THE IMMUNE SYSTEM

In his research on the fight-or-flight response, Dr. Selye noticed the harmful effects of stress on the immune system. More recently, studies have suggested that as many as 90 percent of office visits to primary care physicians are connected to stress. As far as children go, the same is true. A study done by researchers at the University of California found that many children who get sick are victims of stress. The study also found that some youngsters are more sensitive to stress than others and that those youngsters report more illness than others. The same researchers say that finding a way to cope with stress can make the difference in children's physical well-being. New research has also substantiated the notion of the so-called stress cold. Yes, studies show that stress can inhibit your immune system and make you more vulnerable to a cold. In fact, one study by psychologists at Carnegie-Mellon University and the University of Pittsburgh School of Medicine found that *chronic* stress (meaning stress that lasts more than a month) more than doubles a person's *risk* of developing cold symptoms, and *acute* stress (sudden, short-term, intense stress) actually *triggers* the colds (whose symptoms show up three to five days later.)

How is it that stress can take such a toll? Well, remember what I was saying earlier about stress hormones slowing down digestion. It turns out that the stress response also slows down or exhausts many other body functions that don't specifically relate to repelling the perceived threat. Unfortunately, one of those functions happens to be your immune system. Hormones produced under stress can eventually repress certain white blood cells that help promote immunity. If the stress is constant and long-term, so are the harmful effects on the immune system.

In the same way that stress can bring on a cold that's already brewing, it can also exacerbate other preexisting conditions in your child's body. Here's a list of various diseases, disorders, and ailments that can get worse when your child is under chronic stress:

> Ulcerative colitis
> Peptic ulcers
> Irritable bowel syndrome
> Hyperventilation
> Asthma
> Rheumatoid arthritis
> Allergies
> Skin disorders

If you do become aware of direct associations between stress and the exacerbation of preexisting conditions in your child, you should check with your child's doctor. Parents, of course, can add many other physiological symptoms that are not generally documented but that get worse when their child is under either short- or long-term stress. Though such symptoms may be classified as less serious by medical professionals, you will not think there is anything less serious about them when you see your child suffering from them. These symptoms include the following:

> Headaches
> Swallowing difficulties
> Nausea
> Heartburn (hyperacidity)
> Cold sweats
> Stomach knots and butterflies
> Neck aches
> Chronic fatigue
> Dizziness
> Chest pains
> Backaches
> Urinary frequency
> Muscle spasms
> Memory loss
> Panic attacks
> Constipation
> Diarrhea
> Insomnia

Perhaps one of the most serious potential effects of kidstress is a slowdown of growth. Here's how doctors say it can work. The pituitary gland, the master endocrine or hormone gland, is connected to the brain through nerves and chemicals, and therefore affects virtually every bodily function. One of the important hormones the pituitary sends into the bloodstream is known as the growth hormone. This hormone helps the body synthesize protein and manufacture tissue, directly stimulating the timing and extent of growth, most noticeable during infancy and early childhood as skeletal and muscle systems go through growth spurts. But adrenaline, the stress hormone, triggers the release of norepinephrine, which travels to the same part of the pituitary that makes growth hormones. Essentially, the pituitary, which has limited capability, cuts back on the long-term hormonal needs of tissue development and pumps adrenaline to the short-term emergency. Enough continuing stress, and a resulting hormonal imbalance can affect a child's physical development. Your family physician can tell you more, if you are concerned about this possibility.

INDIVIDUAL DIFFERENCES

One stressful situation, three different children, three different reactions. Teachers and parents see this every day. One cries, another laughs, a third gets a stomachache. No two children will deal with the same situation in exactly the same way. Each child is born with his or her own individual coping style. The watchful parent can detect his child's "stress style" from the earliest age. Check out your baby in the crib. Does she fuss, turn, cry, and wail until you pick her up? Does she move and pull and push all day? Or is she content to play with her fingers and nurse? Many mothers say they are aware of their baby's temperament even before the baby is born. That fusser, for instance, kept kicking around in utero, according to her mother. And the placid baby was as docile prenatally as she was after she was born. These temperamental differences may be due to differences in metabolism, body type, brain biochemistry, or body chemistry.

Aside from how each child's own body influences his or her response to stress, the child's thinking can play as large a role—if not larger. Different children have different "thinking styles." Parents who recognize their child's problem-solving style can help that child develop his capacity. Parents who don't, may try to force an incompatible style on him. For example, most kids are either divergent or convergent thinkers. Divergent thinkers are good at expansive thinking, good at finding new uses for an old toy or tool or piece of information. In a stressful situation, for example, a divergent thinker would draw from her previous experiences something she knows she can do and reapply it in a new and creative way. She'd use her pencil as a splint if a plant was tilting on her windowsill, or use her fishing skills to retrieve a key she dropped between two boxes too heavy to move. If you want to see whether your child is a divergent thinker, put a plain red brick on the table. Ask your child to suggest as many different things as possible that it could be used for. Start it off: it could be a paperweight or the base of a lamp. A divergent thinker will come up with tons of possibilities and may grow up to be an artist, designer, or other creative type.

A convergent thinker, on the other hand, is good at synthesizing, bringing many separate elements together in a new way. Under stress, he would focus on the dilemma until he saw it in a new way, more clearly—converging his idea onto one point. Like a detective or a scientist, he could create a theory from lots of scattered clues. A convergent thinker can figure out a plan of action when the group is lost in the woods or on the wrong bus, or he can finish a jigsaw puzzle in record time. My daughter, a classic convergent thinker, made to-do lists by the time she was in third grade and uses her jigsaw-puzzle and list-making skills today as a trial lawyer. Convergent problem solvers make great office managers and organizational specialists—and trial lawyers.

You'll know early on what type of child you have. Your mission is to learn as much as you can about what type your child is, as early as you can, and then work with your child in finding the ways to best cope with all the different kinds of stress he or she will face in life. It may be a learn-by-your-mistakes process. But with luck, patience, and perseverance (on both your part and your child's), you will be able to help your child learn how to get through any stressful event life throws at him or her.

NATURE AND NURTURE

Two ingredients go into the development of a child's personality. One is your child's temperament, which we just discussed. Studies have found that temperament is largely "nature," obvious from birth and pretty constant throughout our lives. If you're a parent, you probably suspected this all along—three children, all different from the day they were born. An easygoing baby, a high-strung baby, an outgoing baby—all seem to influence their parents' reactions as much as parents influence theirs. One long-term study of twins raised apart estimated that about half of the variables in their stress reactions were inborn.

The other ingredient is what children learn, how they are taught to "be" by both their caretakers and the environment in which they grow up. The most influential people in that environment are parents, but others also leave strong positive impressions: brothers, sisters, grandparents, aunts, uncles, cousins, and friends. There are also teachers and mentors, plus influences they will never meet: TV and film heroes, comic-strip characters, princes and princesses, and other admirable characters they will, hopefully, encounter in literature. If these people who dot a child's landscape are positive role models, the child is lucky. Such, however, is not always the case. And, unfortunately, a child's environment can never be completely under a parent's control.

The part of the environment that you can control, however—your own behavior—has been shown to play a very large role. Even the notorious terrible twos are not all caused by a child's "nature." Nurture is a factor. A study by researchers at

Pennsylvania State University found that whether a child has a full-blown case of the terrible twos has as much to do with the stress and anxiety in the parents' lives as with the child's innate temperament or developmental stage. Looking at sixty-nine families with first-born sons, they found every child had some episode of terrible twos between the ages of fifteen months and thirty-three months. But they found that, of the fifteen families with sons who acted out the most, the problems were usually made worse when

- Parents were more anxious, depressed, and hostile, and less sociable and friendly.
- Families had lots of work-related stress.
- Families had fewer economic resources.

GENDER AND STRESS

Since we're talking about the influence of nature and nurture, let's discuss gender.

There's just no escaping it. Despite years of controversy and debate about if, how, and why boys and girls are different, the bottom line is that boys and girls often do behave quite differently. And though generalizations are often dangerous, parents and health professionals see evidence that those differences mean that each gender will deal with stress in different ways.

Sure, every child is unique. Sure, there are exceptions to the rule. Yes, some boys are quiet, passive, and highly verbal. Some would even rather play with a cuddly doll than an erector set. True, some girls are naturally athletic, are great at math and the sciences, and like to fix and build things.

But by and large, the gender stereotypes we hear about are based on observation. As early as in the maternity ward, parents and nurses detect girls generally behaving differently from boys. And as they grow, we see many more examples of those differences. Even when parents try to raise their children without gender bias, they still often report that their children show certain gender-specific tendencies. Parents say that:

- Girls tend to agree more readily than boys; they offer to do things for people more frequently.
- Girls seem more concerned than boys with social relationships and with how they look.
- Girls get anxious more frequently than boys.
- Girls rely on their intuitive abilities more than boys.
- Girls are more verbal at a younger age than boys; they start to speak and develop reading skills younger.
- Girls respond to emotional cues—their own and others'—more than boys do.
- Girls' fine-motor coordination is better developed than boys'.
- Boys are physically stronger than girls.
- Boys are generally more aggressive and impulsive.
- Boys tend to be more active.
- Boys are more independent at an earlier age than girls.
- Boys tend to take things apart and try to to put them back together again.
- Boys seem to get less sleepy, stay awake longer, and nap less.
- Boys prefer to play with "masculine" toys like tanks.

How much of these behaviors can be attributed to physical differences? How much has to do with the different ways we treat girls and boys—that is, how much is the result of social conditioning? How much is nature? How much is nurture? How much has to do with genetic differences, and how much with the environment in which we raise children? How much has to do with the models of "femininity" and "masculinity" we present to youngsters and then reinforce by our behaviors (and that are reinforced in films, books, and other societal influences)?

I'm afraid the answers are not simple. It's difficult to separate the influences of nature and nurture. This may well be like the chicken-or-egg question. Which came first? Are little girls more social and verbal because we talk to them more, or do we talk to them more because they are social and verbal? As is often noted, some of those differences between boys and girls may be due to social conditioning. When we see a girl, we cuddle her; when we see a boy, we play-wrestle with him. We give a girl a doll; we give a boy building blocks. Little surprise, then, that she wants to be a nurturer and he wants to build empires. Do we actually treat girls and boys differently because their own behavior evokes these responses from us? There is a large and growing body of research that is seeking the answer to such questions. Let's look at a few of these studies and see what they suggest.

EARLY SOCIALIZATION IN GIRLS

Sexual stereotypes are well ingrained in parents. Even before our baby is born, preconceived notions influence how we will treat him or her. In one classic study of 110 cultures, psychologists found that 82 percent of the people they polled expected females to be more nurturing than males; 87 percent expected females to be less achievement oriented than males; and 85 percent expected females to be less self-reliant than males. In another survey, psychologists concluded that fathers expect daughters to be pretty, sweet, and fragile and that they expect sons to be aggressive and athletic.

Such expectations may create a self-fulfilling prophecy. What we see—or expect to see—is what we'll get. In one study that corroborates that idea, researchers showed men videotapes of seventeen-month-old babies. When told they were looking at a boy, the men were more likely to describe the child as active, alert, and aggressive. When told they were looking at a girl, they saw the very same child as passive and delicate.

Children often mirror the expectations we have of them. They turn our projections into reality. For example, research finds:

- Most girls are treated more protectively than boys. That may suggest to them that they need to be protected.
- Girls' appearance is commented on more frequently than any other trait. That may reinforce the idea that they are judged by how they look.
- Adults communicate verbally more with girls than they do with boys. One study found that mothers respond more to the babbling of twelve-week-old girl babies than they do to that of same-aged boy babies. Another study found the same true of fathers. Such responses may tell girls that they are expected to communicate.
- The cross-cultural study mentioned above found that fathers emphasized assertion, aggression, achievement, and self-aggrandizement in their sons, but stressed control of aggression and assertion in their daughters. This probably encourages girls to live up to that old verse about "sugar and spice and everything nice."
- A study found that mothers of kindergarten children tolerate their daughters' aggressiveness toward parents and peers less than their sons'. The same was

found in a separate study of nursery school teachers. This may remind girls to behave in school and, more than boys, they do.

These studies suggest that even if girls do have some natural capacity for self-control and communication, these traits are certainly also reinforced by *our* behavior. That's what social conditioning is. But the next question we have to ask is this: How does this affect girls when they are under stress?

THE STRESSFUL PRICE OF GIRLS' SELF-CONTROL

Whether it's nature or nurture or both, by the time girls are just eighteen months old, they already control their tempers more often than boys do. But girls can pay a price for this self-control.

When we fear internal impulses such as anger—or other emotions that someone else has deemed "unacceptable"—that fear is called anxiety. Girls who keep being told they should control their natural feelings of aggressiveness, assertiveness, or ambition may develop various levels of anxiety as they struggle to suppress those feelings. Girls who are told those impulses are undesirable, bad, or not the way "young ladies" act may feel guilty and try to avoid those feelings and, again, feel that fear of their own impulses called anxiety. Studies seem to confirm this. On a number of measures, anxiety scores for girls were higher than boys among groups of French, African American, and American children and among groups of girls from age thirteen through college.

There are times, of course, when controlling our emotions is a healthy and mature strategy for coping with stress. But how much is too much? Repressing strong emotional impulses can put great strain on both body and mind.

One striking, large study actually linked emotional problems in girls to stunted growth. It showed that adolescent and preteen girls who were overly anxious grew up to be an average of one to two inches shorter than other girls. When the researchers couldn't find a similar association among boys, they concluded it was because boys are less likely to have emotional conflicts. The larger implication of the study was that anxiety and depression may, under certain conditions, suppress growth hormones, resulting in smaller bones and muscles. What fascinated the chairman of an American Academy of Pediatrics committee on psychosocial health about this study was "the connection it shows between emotional disorders and the neuro-endocrine systems." In other words, mental stress stresses the body, too.

GIRLS' SUCCESS STRESS

As strange as it may seem, even at the end of the enlightened twentieth century, girls still get mixed messages when it comes to success and failure. They are encouraged to compete and achieve academically at the highest levels. Yet when they do, they are still sometimes dubbed "too smart" or "too strong," or later in their careers they're pigeonholed as "too pushy" or "too manipulative."

There are many exceptions to the rule, but that's just it: Janet Reno, Elizabeth Dole, and Sally Ride are considered uncommon women. These are women whose need for achievement may have won out over any fear of failure. For we all—male or female—have a desire to achieve, to exert control over situations, and to solve problems.

For girls and women, though, it's not uncommon to feel both a fear of failure and a need for achievement at the same time. And it's the collision of those two impulses that aggravates what I have called the female stress syndrome. Stress affects not only females' bodies but also their minds. Not only can it trigger physical symptoms—like headaches, fatigue, backaches, colds, and chronic intestinal problems—but it can also trigger emotional symptoms like nervousness, insecurity, and anxiety.

To deal with the conflict between desire for success and fear of failure, some girls learn to do everything the hard way: they overcommit their time, do too many things simultaneously, and try to be all things to all people. That way, they have an excuse in case they fail, and they have less guilt about their hard-won successes.

As a parent, you can help your young girl from an early age build constructive skills to cope with stress. In the following chapters, you'll find a wide variety of techniques.

IT'S A BOY

When did you first notice that your son was different from your daughter? Was it, Mom, while you were pregnant? Did he seem to kick and fidget a great deal? Or, Dad, was it in the maternity ward? Was your son turning more than the girls around him?

The average American male weighs 7.5 pounds at birth, a half pound heavier than the average newborn female. His heart and lungs are larger too, and he's usually born earlier in the cycle—already the impatient, rambunctious lad. He has more testosterone, the hormone that eventually regulates secondary sex characteristics such as facial hair and muscle growth and that helps fuel the sex drive. He startles more easily than girls and makes more movements per second. He is at higher risk of death by miscarriage or at birth than females. Though both men and women live longer than they used to, it's still men who die younger than women.

Along with the physical differences, there are some semi-predictable behavioral differences. As I suggested earlier about girls, it's hard to say whether we socialize and reinforce behaviors that become known as male or whether we're just responding to their natural inclinations. Either way, as the saying goes, boys will be boys. Along with the different expectations parents have of boys, mentioned earlier in this chapter, parents also handle boys differently, as developmental psychologists have found. Some examples:

- Fathers will roughhouse with their infant sons more than with their infant daughters.
- Both mothers and fathers respond less to their infant son's vocalizations than to their daughter's. They do respond more to his attempts to grasp, crawl, and walk.
- Parents allow boys to roam farther than girls on playgrounds and in yards.
- Parents more readily push boys into activities that frighten them than they push girls.

CHIP OFF THE OLD BLOCK

Girls tend to copy their moms; boys tend to mimic their dads. It's often true: like father, like son. Men need to keep this in mind. In many families, the father may well not be around as much as mothers, but, Dad, no matter how much you're around, your influence is very powerful. Even your absence makes an impression. In studies I examined, boys whose fathers were absent for various lengths of time from birth to adolescence were less assertive, more dependent, more submissive, and less secure in their masculinity than boys whose fathers were present. In one study, recreational directors rated nine- to twelve-year-olds whose fathers had been absent since their fourth year and found them to be more dependent on their peers and less likely to engage in physical contact games than boys whose fathers were present. Ten- to thirteen-year-old boys without fathers scored lower on academic tests than classmates with fathers. Boys without fathers had more difficulties in self-control. And a team of psychologists observed that rebelliousness against and a rejection of male authority figures were more characteristic among adolescent boys whose fathers were absent.

Although more fathers today are choosing to be more participatory as parents, I found one study that convinced me that too many fathers still spend too little time alone with their sons. In this study, a group of 300 seventh- and eighth-grade boys were asked to keep a careful record of the time they spent alone with their fathers over a two-week period. The results: the average time each boy spent alone with his father was seven and a half minutes each week!

The effect of this is that many sons wander through life without strong, present, positive male role models. On many levels, this can cause great stress for a boy. Therefore, one simple way a father, uncle, brother, or grandfather can start to help reduce a boy's stress might be to just spend more time with him.

FATHERS AND SONS: A STRESSFUL RELATIONSHIP

Of course, it's not all that simple. In fact, fathers can be the source of a great deal of stress, especially to a boy. While the stress in a girl's life most often has to do with overcoming the conflicting fear of failure and fear of success, a boy's challenge is often to live up to the image of the man who is, in his eyes, Superman. Imagine the stress of having to measure up to a man who is bigger, stronger, wiser, and more powerful, and with whom he must share the only woman in his life, Mom. No wonder so many young men have such ambivalent relationships with their fathers. No wonder a father's acceptance, approval, and involvement mean so much.

Fathers of high-achieving boys who take stress in stride are often competent men willing to take a back seat while their sons are performing—"beckoning from ahead rather than pushing from behind," as one researcher put it. This quality presumably also helps a boy develop a sense of self-reliance.

But it also puts a great deal of stress on a boy as he enters puberty and begins to understand that his worth as a man will be determined by how well he exerts control, takes charge, beats out the other guy for the job, the woman, the whatever.

There is some good news here, however, in the complex and stressful world of fathers and sons. Of late, there is a new type of father, a father who chooses to spend time with his children, a father who chooses to nurture them, a father who expresses his love both by saying it and by demonstrating it. Fathers who think that the way to teach their sons to be "real men" is to be tough, hard disciplinarians without showing their softer side are mistaken, as shown by three researchers in separate studies. They found that the more the father metes out love and praise as well as punishment, the more of an influence he will have on his son. Hugging, sharing quality time, and expressing sympathy for the difficulties a boy may be going through—these are powerful antidotes to the stresses that will naturally be part of that boy's life.

MEDIA HEROES:
THE OTHER MALE ROLE MODELS

In the absence of fathers or even father figures—male teachers, coaches, uncles, mentors—many boys turn to the images that wallpaper all our lives: the men in films, on TV, in advertisements, books, and magazines.

I'd like to say that the media offer boys a healthy and positive image of masculinity, as well as a vision of how to deal successfully with stress. But for the most part, films, TV, ads, and commercials often serve up cartoon-like caricatures. "Action heroes" was the term coined in the 1990s to refer to the characters played by such box-office stars as Claude Van Damm, Sylvester Stallone, Steven Segal, Chuck Norris, and Arnold Schwarzenegger. They are the descendants of another generation's John Wayne, Gary Cooper, Errol Flynn, William S. Hart, and Tom Mix. They are all powerful characters who show little true emotion, who live up to their billing: they are men of action. They do now, think later. Men of few words, they often let their violent actions speak for them while their motives get lost in the smoke of exploding helicopters, bridges, jeeps, and other large objects.

And how do these action characters deal with stress? Usually by blasting their Uzis into a crowd or bashing their fists through a wall or numbing their brains at a bar. These are the behaviors of what has come to be known and admired by both men and women as "the strong, silent type." And those are models of male behavior that die hard. Sometimes literally.

What boys remember most from a typical action movie is that the aggressive, assertive, self-assured violent guy appears to win the money, the war, the woman, and, in the boys' (and the filmmaker's) eyes, the respect of everyone.

The violence makes an impression. Or, that is, many impressions. One study of violence in the media found that, by the age of ten, the average child will have seen the destruction of more than six thousand people on TV. By fifteen, the teenager will have witnessed some thirteen thousand violent TV deaths. In the 1970s, the surgeon general linked the watching of television to aggressive behavior. In the 1990s, parents watching their boys after they've watched Saturday-morning action cartoons can make the same link.

A pair of social psychologists in the 1960s found that 79 percent of children who watched a cartoon with aggression and violence imitated some of the same behaviors while playing afterward. More recently, in 1993 the American Psychological Association's Commission on Violence reported that viewing violence increases violence and leads to emotional desensitization toward violence. In other words, if you watch a lot of killing and other forms of man's inhumanity toward man, soon you can begin to take it for granted. In another unsettling study that involved 875 children and covered twenty-two years from the time they were eight years old, boys who were not usually aggressive but who watched great amounts of violent TV programming grew up to be as violence-prone as the eight-year-olds who were the most aggressive school bullies.

BALANCING THE STRESS OF VIOLENCE

In the face of all this unsavory modeling of violence, especially in the case of those boys who may have a problem controlling aggressive behavior, what's a parent to do? One thing to remember is that, for a boy, Dad (or a male equivalent) is still the first and primary male role model. When it comes to handling stress, a boy tends to follow in his father figure's footsteps. The father who comes home from a tough day at work and kicks the dogs, as one child who answered the KidStress Survey put it, should not be surprised to see similar behavior being tried by his son. When Johnny is losing at checkers, does he knock over the board? When he comes home with poor grades, does he terrorize his sister? If his friends reject him, does he retreat to his room for long periods of time?

On the other hand, the father who sets a good example will be training his son to deal with the natural stressors in life and to combat the violent media images he will not be able to avoid. Teach your son some of your healthy coping strategies, and not only will you give him lifelong tools for living but you will also probably nurture a lifelong friendship that will transcend even the turbulent teenage years of rebellion. Take him on a hike in the woods, join a tai chi class together, introduce him to a hobby, go jogging together. These are the lessons that will have as much, if not more, enduring meaning as teaching him how to change the oil or tip a waitress. Here are a couple more suggestions:

Let Him Cry. Being afraid is not "unmanly." Crying can be okay when you're frightened or worried. It's even okay at the end of some sentimental movie about a lost dog. Give him permission to have feelings. If you limit the bounds of his emotional expressiveness, you also limit his creativity, his ability to reach out to other people, and his ability to understand his own feelings.

Emphasize Process, Not Product. One of the big stressors in a boy's life is performance. While some women explain that they feel like sex objects, society makes some men say they feel like success objects. They are under pressure to reach that goal, whether it's the touchdown or the sales quota. Here's your opportunity to use all those clichés: "It's not whether you win or lose, it's how you play the game"; "The secret of life is to enjoy the passage of time." Give your young sons A's for effort.

Reinforce Mastery, Not Competition. It's natural for fathers to teach their sons skills—fixing things, throwing balls, driving cars. But make sure the focus is on the fun of learning and not on becoming better than someone else.

Let Him Go, Let Him Come Back. Society seems to admire independent men. When boys begin to separate from their parents, often it's under societal pressure. Sometimes, when the separation comes too soon or the going alone gets too tough, boys may want to come back into the family fold for a while. Let them. And make sure they understand it's not a failure to want or need your support from time to time.

Show Him How to Nurture. Boyhood should not be all sticks and stones. Every now and then little boys—and even not-so-little boys—like affection. If they won't come out and ask for displays of affection, you have to find subtle ways to make them available. Someday your son may be a father himself. Hopefully, with you as a model, he will be a father who knows how to nurture as well as to pitch a strike ball.

WHAT'S A PARENT TO DO?

Nature versus nurture. As I said earlier, it's an old debate about which has more influence. To me, they both must be factored in when you look at the whole child, because a child's nature is influenced by how he or she is nurtured. Each child is born with her own temperament and her own set of capacities for dealing with stress. This is what we call her "nature," and we as parents can usually do very little to alter it. But what we *can* do as parents is to influence the environment in which our children grow up. We can help nurture our children in a variety of styles that complement their own natural tendencies. We can teach them how to begin to manage their temperament and their environment so that they grow up capable of handling stress in the healthiest manner possible.

Throughout the rest of this book, I'll continue to emphasize the interlocking relationship between nature and nurture. I'll also show you how to intervene where and when possible, and how to encourage your child's own natural stress-coping capacities.

THE SIGNS OF STRESS IN CHILDREN

By now you should have a sense of how stress works, and how it differs in girls and boys, but how do you know when it is taking its toll? What are the emotional, physical, and behavioral signs of stress in children?

It's not easy, because children have a stress language all their own. In fact, it often seems that each child speaks in a dialect known only to him or her. Our job as parents is to interpret and understand our children's special stress vocabulary even though much of what kids tell us is nonverbal: not with words.

They talk to us through their behavior, their emotions, and in body language. We begin to "hear" what they are trying to tell us from their very earliest days. That is, we learn to "listen" with our eyes and other senses; we "hear" them with our minds, our intuition, and our hearts.

We begin to know how they are feeling and what they are feeling by recognizing a look in their eyes (scared, happy, content, mischievous), by studying the muscles in their face (angry, nervous, relaxed), by noticing how they are holding their bodies (depressed, confident, sick in the stomach), or even by hearing the tone of their voice or the sound of their cry (tired, bored, hungry).

This dialogue between parents and child starts in the crib (though some mothers say their infants speak to them even before they are born). At each age and stage from then on, we learn to pick up cues and messages that convey to us their needs and wants, their moods, their aches and pains, and their worries and their fears—as well as their excitement, contentment, and happiness.

Though children do not come with an owner's manual, you don't have to have a Ph.D. in nonverbal communication to become an expert in your child's body language, especially when he is speaking in the body language of stress. It's a matter of learning how to connect the dots. Just notice how he looks or acts when you know he is feeling stress. The second time you see that same signal in a similar situation should be enough to let you know this is his way of saying "This situation is overwhelming my body and my mind, and if you and I don't figure out a way to either end the situation or help me cope with it, I will keep on feeling this way."

PHYSICAL SYMPTOMS

As you read in chapter 2, when children were asked to identify their physical reactions to stress, the three most frequently reported responses were insomnia (47 percent), stomachaches (44 percent), and "feeling sick" (26 percent). Headaches came in fourth, with 21 percent, and 9 percent said they felt jumpy.

As just one example, I was amazed at the variety with which children could describe gastrointestinal problems:

"I get a tight knot in my stomach."

"My stomach kills."

"My stomach always hurts."

"My stomach feels weird."

"I pull my hair out and I have indigestion."

"My stomach feels like it is being eaten away by acid.
    I can practically feel the deterioration."

"My stomach gets empty like I feel there is nothing in it."

"My stomach turns in circles."

But they were equally colorful in detailing other effects of stress on their bodies:

"I just start aching all over."

"I'm jumpy, grumpy, unhappy (that's why I go to a shrink)."

"It just feels like something nagging at my heart."

"I just get real scared and hide."

"My heart beats fast."

"Asthma, a huge headache to where if I even move it hurts
    worse, stomach hurts."

"Well, I usually feel really shaky, and a lot of the time I get
    dizzy. I also start shaking my leg, spacing out, doing really
    dumb things, and babbling on about nothing (although I
    do that a lot of the time anyway)."

"I start jumping up and down and screaming at the top of my
    lungs until I pass out."

"Sweating, rubber legs."

"My neck gets hot, my ears get red, and my cheeks burn."

"I play with my lip, and hit my sister."

"I always fiddle with something or become very
    sarcastic."

"I feel funny all over."

"I start to drum my fingers."

Many children will develop their own variations on these themes. They will develop physical tics and quirks and rashes in response to stress. Stress symptoms include

- Frequent colds
- Worsening of existing chronic physical conditions
- Neck and head muscle tension
- Dry mouth
- Sweaty palms
- Trouble waking up
- Excessive or diminished hunger

Be alert for these symptoms, but also be aware that they are not always indicators of stress. If any of these physical ailments persist, I recommend taking your child to a physician. If there are psychological conditions that continue, ask your family doctor for the name of a psychologist or other mental health professional.

BEHAVIORAL SYMPTOMS

Most children have an extraordinary amount of energy. When the fight-or-flight response pumps the hormone adrenaline into their little bodies, they've got even more energy. But unlike adults, who may have learned how to channel that energy productively or at least have developed various coping strategies, children "act up," as we say. They are like small pumps about to explode. With more energy than they know what to do with, they resort to their own strategies in an effort to burn off that energy. Maybe you've recognized some of these attempts:

- Tantrums in preschool, disorderly conduct in older children.

- Behavioral regression (baby-like behavior).
- Moodiness, irritability.
- Social withdrawal, sulking.
- Picking on siblings, fighting.
- Refusing to go to school or day care.
- Distracted concentration.
- Excessive whining and crying.
- Frequent daydreaming.
- Restlessness.

Here's how some kids put these symptoms in their own words:

"I feel light-headed or hot."
"Sweaty palms, racing heart, hands and knees shake."
"Bad headaches, restless, depressed feeling."
"My head hurts and I sleep a lot."
"I feel weak."
"Night terrors."
"Crying, stomachache, asthma attack."
"I feel really tired and I get quiet."
"I get real bad headaches when me and my mom fight . . . I also lose my appetite."
"I tend to bite my nails."
"I bite my nails and start itching."
"If I hear something I get nervous. I guess you could call me jumpy."
"If I am nervous I get clammy."
"I want to be alone."
"Sometimes if I become too nervous or if I am worried about someone, I begin to shake nonstop."

In the survey, as you'll recall from chapter 2, when we gave them a list of behaviors to choose from, the highest percentage of children (65 percent) told us they withdraw in response to stress. That was followed in order by fight with siblings (60 percent), bite nails (50 percent), have trouble sleeping (47 percent), cry easily (43 percent), and have trouble concentrating on homework (41 percent). For the most part, parents who responded to the poll predicted with some accuracy the behaviors they thought their children would name—at least the behaviors that are easily observable. But parents seem to have more difficulty identifying the more subtle cues, particularly withdrawal and daydreaming. This is where my suggestion of learning how to connect the dots may help parents become more attuned to the relationship between their child's behavior and stress. If you notice your child withdrawing with some frequency in response to stressful situations, for example, you can begin to feel confident that that's her "stress-strategy." Then, you can help her replace it with a more effective coping technique.

EMOTIONAL SYMPTOMS

Some of children's behavioral responses to stress are giveaways to their emotional responses. Regression, withdrawal, irritability, disorderly conduct, and picking on siblings, for example, usually mean fear, anger, sadness, or depression. What concerns me most is how few parents are making the connection between emotional symptoms and stress behaviors. It's as though parents don't understand that stress takes a severe emotional toll on children. They may know from firsthand experience that stress can play havoc with adults' emotions, but many perhaps underplay their children's emotions. But kids "act out" stress with bursts of energy, crying, and other external behaviors. If children could put it in sophisticated language, they would be talking about many of the same emotional problems their parents suffer under stress.

KIDS' OWN STRESS-BUSTERS

Knowing what a child is capable of at different developmental stages will help you help your children exercise their stress-coping capacities.

Preschoolers. For example, preschoolers (ages three and a half to five) have not yet mastered logic. They don't understand cause and effect, or sequence. No matter how clever or bright they are, their ability to reason is limited. It would be a waste of time to try to explain to them the relationship between their crying fit and stress. Also, because they have limited memory, trying to explain to them that they acted the same way last week under the same circumstances will also fall on deaf ears.

What preschoolers *can* do is pretend. That's the coping skill you can help them use. With their power to turn a broom into a magic wand, they can also, for example, turn a stress-producing crowded train into a truck full of friendly stuffed animals. They can practice coping skills in their own bedrooms, turning the bedroom floor into a raging ocean and their bed into a protective island. Their imagination is their ticket out of stress. When they grow up and commute on a crowded train, they can draw on the same skills they used as preschoolers, and call it "imagery."

By the age of four, children have developed to the point where they can remember short lists. You can say, "Go to your room, pick up your clothes, put them in the laundry room, and come in for lunch," and they will probably be able to execute those tasks. Similarly, you can suggest a series of mentally and physically demanding exercises to distract them from stress. But remember that even at this age children will still confuse appearances with reality and, with their active imaginations, a coat thrown over a chair will cast a shadow that looks to them like a ghost. It would not be fair to them to call this reaction silly. It's simply how their brains work.

By age four or five, children have a firm command of speech. They will begin to try to put into their own words how stress is affecting them. They may not yet say "stress," but they are likely to use words like "scared" or "feel bad." Learn their language. They will also play-act what they're feeling. Pay attention to the various roles they assign; often those roles will reflect how they feel about you—and themselves. At this age children also begin to group people and experiences. If, for example, they start to exhibit stress symptoms on the drive to Uncle Harry's house, you may guess that they fear Uncle Harry's dog.

Middle Childhood. From five to eight, memory develops more dramatically. A child will be able to remember previous difficult situations—like meeting Uncle Harry's dog—but will begin to apply some solutions that they learned earlier. (They can wait until the dog is put outside before they go into the house.)

One of our greatest stress-coping capacities really begins to develop at this age: humor. The love and appreciation of jokes, riddles, cartoons, and comics enter a child's world with a great pratfall. Parents should key in to their *child's* sense of humor; don't force a grown-up's brand of funny on them—it won't get a laugh! A child's pleasure in humor should not be underestimated. It represents a sophisticated and subtle skill. Understanding a good joke reflects an ability to understand the difference between how people are supposed to act and how they do act. It teaches that unpredictability is funny, not scary. That's a big step for a child who likes things the way they are and gets nervous when things change. Laughing at change gives children (and adults) a sense of control; they see change as part of life.

At age seven, children reach another major turning point

when it comes to coping with stress. They learn that they can predict what will happen in the future based on what happened in the past. This means they now can use logic and reason in solving problems. They move from the immediate and concrete to the hypothetical and abstract. This is the age when they can devise stress-coping skills based on past experiences and apply them to similar encounters in the future.

Here, too, there's a leap forward in children's ability to pay attention for longer periods of time. Their sensory perception and motor coordination become more refined. If a child seems to enjoy playing cards as a stress-coping skill, he can concentrate on the game longer. Of if he likes sports, he'll be more able to distract himself playing catch. Each child will develop his own style: some will read, others will build model airplanes, still others will lose themselves in video games. To each his own!

Children in these middle years also develop social skills that help them cope with people who are different from them. In first and second grade, they learn how to behave in group situations. As a coping skill this can work both for and against them, depending on how well they learn to interact and on their own nature. For children who socialize well, group experiences can serve to help allay stress. For those who act aggressively and antisocially, social situations will produce more stress. It's up to parents to notice their own child's inclinations and respond in a helpful way.

At this age children's personal styles will come out. Some kids look to others for help, whether from peers or adults. Others look within. Keep in mind that one style is not better than the other; they're just different. For each child, it would help to learn to balance. The introvert needs to be slowly introduced to the concept that she can't solve every problem alone, that it's okay to ask for help. The child who looks to others for help should be reminded that she has opportunities to do things on her own, and to enjoy the independence.

Preteens. Children at ten, eleven, and twelve refine their ability to think logically and can work through hypothetical situations more adeptly than younger children. This is a time to set up "what if" situations. If you're helping your kids prepare to undertake a potentially stressful situation—like walking to school alone—ask a series of questions: What if you get lost? What if a stranger approaches you? What if you have to go to the bathroom? Let them come up with solutions or help them find solutions; it will make them feel that much more in control of the situation.

At this age they will often have an imaginary audience. They study themselves in the mirror, perfecting that curl or practicing that swagger. An imaginary audience can help children rehearse for life, but it can also cause a great deal of self-consciousness. Keep that in mind when they seem to be overly sensitive to stressful moments, especially when they have to actually be in front of a real audience. (Imaginary audiences are so much more forgiving and understanding than real ones!)

In preteen humor, you'll notice more sarcasm than before. Sarcasm directed at adults and their world, especially when shared with peers, reminds young people that they're not alone. Sarcasm undercuts the seriousness of the adult world, a world that scares them. Being sarcastic is a socially acceptable way to vent anger that they have probably picked up from adults. Sarcasm directed at their peers may not be as potent to them as it seems to adults. It's like the fighting that occurs among lion cubs; it's practice. They don't mean it when they say "I hate you" or "You're ugly." But within their peer groups is the only place they can get away with hurling these epithets—most of the taunts are empty, but they help kids find out how far they can go. It's a way kids toughen themselves up for the "real world."

Throughout these stages children may change their coping capacities but not their temperament or style. That's because a child's innate temperament strongly colors how he or she responds to stress. What you saw early in your child's life is probably what you'll get later. Children who seem to swim fairly easily through stress without physical or emotional strain from a very early age will not change much as they move into adolescence and even beyond into adulthood. High-strung, sensitive young children to whom small shifts are big deals that trigger severe stress responses have their work cut out for them throughout their lives. These are the children whose parents can help in learning to deal with stress in a way that allows them to lead productive and fulfilling lives. For parents of children with either temperament, I return to my main theme. Consider it a two-step program, with the following sequence:

1. Know Your Children. Watch your children. Study your children. Become a student of your children. Take notes. Observe their behavior in situations that have the potential to cause them stress. Connect the dots. (Be sure to distinguish between what causes *you* stress and what might cause *them* stress.)

2. Help Your Children Help Themselves. Encourage them, with your help at first, to come up with things *they* can do to make the stress more tolerable. Help them realize that stress is a part of life, that they can't always make the stress go away, and that it's a certainty that you are not always going to be there to make it go away. (As for yourself, make sure you have gotten the message that you are not a bad parent because your kids have stress in their lives. Make sure you understand that you are not responsible for their response to that stress.) The sooner you can help them take responsibility for coping with stress, the sooner they will feel more in control of those very situations that have made them feel out of control. And the sooner they will thank you.

CHAPTER 4

School Stress

Every time he had a test in school, it was the same for Martin. He'd wake up slightly nervous, heart already pounding, overcome by a sense of impending doom. He'd have a minor headache and stiffness in his neck. He wasn't that hungry for breakfast. By the time he'd get in the back seat of the van to be carpooled to school, he'd feel slightly nauseous. On the playground before school opened, he would be too distracted to play with his friends. Once in his seat in class, he'd feel butterflies the size of pterodactyls doing flight patterns around his stomach, and by the time the test started, his head had begun to feel like two rams using his temples for battering practice.

When asked "What kinds of things concern you?" children responding to the KidStress Survey said school was their greatest concern, and grades topped their list of what specifically worries them when they think about school. Here's a sampling of their responses:

"Report cards—school."
"Mostly getting schoolwork in on time, and if I'm gonna get caught."
"Doing well on tests especially, even if I know that I knew everything on the test."
"My grades, disappointing my parents."
"Answering questions wrong."
"I worry about deadlines for projects for school. Usually when I put a project off for a while."

"Failing in school."

"Getting things done at school and other stuff, and being an
    overachiever and a perfectionist."

"Not getting an A on school tests."

"Death, grades."

"If I will get my homework done on time."

"Disappointing my father in school."

School, we adults now realize, is a training ground for life.
We may have long forgotten some of the lessons—what's a
rhomboid, anyway?—but other lessons have stayed with us well
into adulthood. I'm referring specifically here to how we
learned to deal with stress. And guess what? Though years have
passed since you were in school, children today are facing the
same stressors there. Actually, kids today face a lot more school
stress than we ever did. Many baby boomers and post–baby
boomers have instilled in their children such competitiveness
that the pressure to get good grades in order to get into a top-
notch institution of higher learning begins as soon as the kids
start school. And, with downsizing becoming the most frequently used management style of the late twentieth century,
the competition for a decent job underscores such parental
concerns.

A good education is an important thing. Unless you're a
champion figure skater, a six-foot-ten-inch basketball star, or a
trust-fund baby, your education is critical to building the kind
of life that will be fulfilling personally and financially. With this
much riding on how well children perform at school, I'm not
surprised that those who responded to my survey ranked school
as the top cause of stress in their lives.

HOW A PARENT CAN HELP

When your child complains of stomachaches on days you know she has a test, have a little sympathy. The worst thing you can do is to ignore or make light of her complaint. Your child is experiencing a physical symptom brought on by worries about her performance in school, worries you (and the rest of society) may well have inspired.

Yet don't give in to her protestations and automatically allow her to stay home. Once children see that they can avoid the stressor (in this case, school) by playing up their symptoms and playing on your sympathies, they are more likely to repeat the behavior—and not learn to cope with the stress. Be firm on this one. And make it a standing rule in your family: Thou shalt attend school daily unless *truly* ill (or unless there's a major family crisis).

Rather than ignoring or giving in to your child, it would be better to honor her worries by letting her talk about them. Remind her that you, too, were nervous about school. You should also be prepared for the same intensity of stress at the beginning of each new level of school: at the start of middle or junior high school, and again at the start of high school and even college. Educators and parents have found the transition to middle school, though, to be the most stress-inducing, probably because at that stage reality sets in and kids realize their performance is being closely watched and will, to some degree, help determine their future.

Actually, long before your children even start kindergarten, you can help them develop a positive attitude about school. That not only reduces some of their stress but also helps build an anticipatory excitement. While they are still toddlers, use opportunities throughout the day to emphasize how school will make their lives so much more fun. When they want to buy something, talk about how math will help them know whether they have enough money to buy what they want. In the video rental store, point out letters in the film titles and tell them that when they learn to read in school, they'll be able to pick out their own movies. Get an older child (a brother or sister if there is one) to tell them about the fun parts of school, like holiday parties or field trips to see dinosaur bones.

Also involve young children in the preparation for school by taking them shopping for school clothes, helping them organize a notebook, and setting up a desk area in their room. They'll recognize that they're making an effort to get ready and be in control of this new experience. That recognition alone will make them feel better about the unknown that's looming ahead.

You also need to assure your children that although the stress is real, they will eventually adjust to the new surroundings and schedules, the new people, and the new challenges. For most youngsters, the headaches, stomachaches, and other symptoms will soon disappear. For some, it will take longer.

If the symptoms continue or last longer than you feel comfortable with, and reassurances to your child seem to be going nowhere, make an appointment to see the child's teacher or school guidance counselor. And talk to other parents in your child's class to see if their kids are unusually stressed out. The problem may not be your child; sometimes the problem really *is* school.

Is Your Child Ready for School?

It's not hard to relate to a child's anxiety that first day of kindergarten. Your little baby, off on her own! The separation anxiety can be as high for you as it is for her.

Some parents worry that although their child may be intellectually ready for this big step, he is not emotionally ready.

How do you know if your child is mature? The American Academy of Pediatrics has developed some indicators to help parents decide for themselves. The Academy says your child is ready for school if he or she:

- Is in good physical health, sees and hears well.
- Has self-care skills (dressing, eating, washing, toilet training).
- Follows directions, has a good attention span, shares, and takes turns.
- Is able to work independently.
- Tolerates frustration and failure.
- Knows her own full name and that of her parents.
- Easily makes changes and accepts adult supervision and help.
- Plays well in small groups with other children.
- Speaks clearly and demonstrates age-appropriate language skills.

Push a kid into school before he's ready, and you'll put him in a stressful situation in which he always feels as though he's trying to catch up to everyone else. That's not fair to any kid, least of all yours. This is a decision that has to be made on a child-by-child basis. If you think you can't make the decision yourself, talk to the school counselors and psychologists, who may administer tests on your child to help you determine his school readiness.

GREAT EXPECTATIONS: THE FIRST DAY OF SCHOOL

Fear of the unknown is a big part of the stress of starting school. Tell your child as much as you can about what to expect.

Describe the physical setting, explain the schedule, talk about the kinds of things she'll learn, mention friends she'll see there. It's even a good idea to go by the school in late summer, walk the school grounds with her, and, if possible, point out where her classroom will be.

Most important in the beginning: always let your child know who will be there at the other end of his long day (even if it's not at the end of his school day but your work day). By honoring that commitment, you show your child that people will be there when they say they will. And let him know the same is expected of him.

Expect stress symptoms to start cropping up in those weeks and days before school starts. There will be questions about who in the family is where and at what time, and other more global inquiries that won't make sense unless you imagine your child's worry wheels spinning. Has your child gotten testy and moody? Any changes in eating habits or bowel movements? Building up to the first day of school, expect insomnia or troubled sleep, with dreams and nightmares (ask your child if he remembers any dreams from the night before to find out what he may be most worried about).

When that day comes, your palms may be sweating more than your child's. Along with her own anxiety, she picks up your nervousness. Her sweaty hand is wrapped around your sweaty hand as you both enter the classroom. And neither of you wants to let go. That's when the whining, crying, clinging, and stomachaches start—for both of you! You worry that if you leave, your child will cry all day, but that if you stay in the classroom or take your child home you will be spoiling her or encouraging her dependency. What should you do? Consider these suggestions:

- Handle your own stress. Some studies have shown that the more distress parents show, the more distress their kids feel. It makes sense. So as much as possible, put on a brave face, remind yourself that you survived when you were young, and contain your own anxiety—even if it's just an act.

- Don't sneak out of school. How would you feel if someone you loved and trusted disappeared in the middle of a crisis? You'd think they were impolite, not to be trusted—and you wouldn't forget it.

- Don't scold or embarrass. Remember that what they are feeling is very real to children. They are feeling not just the anxiety of the unknown and the scariness of being with strangers, but the fear of abandonment as well. These are instincts of self-protection and not necessarily bad instincts to have. If you scold your child or call him a baby, you'll discourage him from trusting his natural survival nature.

- Pull a switch. Get your child to focus on what she's getting, not what she's giving up. Introduce girls to a teacher you think they may like; point boys in the direction of the fun action toys and building blocks.

- Provide details. Tell your child exactly how long he'll be staying at the school or play group. Tell him exactly where you'll be and what you'll be doing. Tell him exactly when and where you or someone else will pick him up. And then be there!

- Be firm. Assert that you will stay for five minutes but that then you are leaving. Once you say so, try not to back down—that would send the wrong message. If your child is absolutely terrified, wetting her pants, or shaking uncontrollably, of course you must be flexible. But you'll find some relief in knowing that research shows that the amount of carrying on during the first week of school has no correlation with the adjustment the child has made six months later.

- Let Dad be the drop-off specialist if possible. From the mouths of teachers: children cry and fuss less when they're dropped off by their fathers than when dropped off by their mothers. This is one time, Mom, when the expectations of traditional gender roles may work to your advantage.

ON THEIR OWN

Soon that first day of kindergarten or that letting-go ritual each morning at school will seem like a distant memory to your child and you. But next year it may begin anew with another step into independence—and another opportunity to be fearful. This step comes when you say goodbye at your front door and your child walks alone to the school bus or all the way to school.

Many youngsters who take the school bus are struck with fear the second they climb onto that big yellow monster. As a child walks down the aisle looking for a friendly familiar face, mostly what he sees are other scared little faces staring back at him. Or perhaps he sees older kids looking very confident—which only feeds his insecurity—or cliques of kids who ostracize him.

One way to alleviate children's school-bus fears is to have them wait at the stop with a buddy, or meet a friend on board. You can prearrange this with another parent or tell the kids to save each other seats on the bus. You can also try to make friends with the regular driver and make him or her aware that your youngster is new to all this and a little frightened. Introduce your child to the driver; get on a first-name basis if appropriate. If you go to the bus stop with your child the first couple of times, introduce her to other children standing there. Introduce yourself to other parents so that your child sees you acting as a good role model. You can all help one another cope with the stressful situation.

If your child walks to school, before the first day go over the route with him. Walk it with him and remind him of the basics: Look both ways, cross at the crosswalk. Arrange for him to walk with a buddy to school, hopefully an older child.

To prepare your child for those first mornings of getting up earlier than she's used to, start setting the alarm to the new wake-up time at least a week before school actually starts. You could make doctor's appointments or plan other reasons she has to get up—and stay up! Of course, the hard part of this assignment is convincing her to go to sleep the night before at a reasonable "school-night" hour. (For advice on coping with the bedtime blues, see chapter 8.)

Discuss with your child how she can help to prepare her breakfast. Go shopping together so she can pick out breakfast foods she likes that also happen to be healthy—juice, fruit, muffins, sugarless cereals, and milk. Do the same with lunches. Pack what she likes for lunch, but make sure to provide her with healthy fuel to get her through the rest of the day.

How a day starts can set its tone. If everyone is rushing around the house at 7:00 A.M. like mad men and women, with you juggling both yourself and your children, when you get to your desk at 8:30 you'll already feel fatigued. To avoid this, use a twofold approach: prepare in advance as much as you can, and expect the unexpected. Make and pack the sandwiches the night before, but don't have a fit when someone spills the milk because, at some point, someone will spill the milk. So build in time for the unexpected. That way it won't surprise you. Getting to bed on time is a great way to start the next day. Make sure your child respects the importance of bedtime. Explain: "It's not a punishment; it's to give you enough energy to have tons of fun tomorrow."

SCARY CLASSMATES

The social world into which your child is being thrust causes a lot of stress, sometimes more than homework does. Kids can be brutal to each other. And, just as when you were in school, you can be sure every class has (at least) one bully. How well your child deals with the class tough guy or gal will help him when he grows up because, as you also know too well, there are bullies at work, in social circles, and among the bureaucrats and restaurant head waiters you'll deal with throughout life.

No matter what age, bullies are always looking for games to play or wars to wage, even if they're just "play" wars. To help your child learn to deal with such game players, encourage him not to buy in to the game in the first place. That alone may work to discourage the bully; even bullies need a willing partner to play bully with. Tell your child to be firm, to look the bully straight in the eye and say he's neither intimidated nor willing to fight. Another tactic is to completely ignore the taunts of the bully. Tell your child, "You can walk away. Don't incite, don't threaten to get your big brother. Just turn away and don't even acknowledge that you heard the insult."

Still another approach is to suggest that your child stand there and let the bully rant and rave (as long as there's no danger of being hurt). Tell him that if he reacts, he's only empowering the bully. No reaction, no satisfaction! Eventually he'll probably wear the bully down. But tell him that sometimes a bully is dangerous and he must leave the scene as quickly as possible. Forget appearances. Forget defending "manliness" or the "family name." Leave. Remind him that he can't be a victim if he's not there. And a bully can't be a bully without someone to bully.

One study found that the number of primary school children expelled each year has quadrupled since the start of 1990. The majority of the kids were boys, and the main reason for expulsion was physical aggression. And here's the relevant kicker: in examining those expelled, the lead researcher said, "What we found was an awful lot of stress." So give a copy of this book to the parents of school bullies—they're the ones who need to find better ways to help their kids deal with stress.

We can endlessly debate why physically aggressive behavior exists among children. One explanation is that American children witness eight thousand murders on television and one hundred thousand other violent acts before they reach junior high school, according to a survey by the American Psychological Association. You can also blame the economy. Children from poor or marginalized families who have lost hope for the bright future they keep seeing promised are unconcerned about the consequences of violence, according to a director of the National School Boards Association, which conducted a nationwide study of violence in schools.

Regardless of the causes, and unless there is a sudden, wide-scale sociological change, we must teach our children how to deal with those who are aggressive. Try suggesting some of these possibilities to your child:

- Don't draw attention to yourself. At least, don't go out of your way to incite problems. Wearing colors you know are associated with a local gang is not a smart idea. Taunting a gang of bullies just so you can ignore them when they threaten you is not wise either.
- Don't go alone. Travel in pairs or groups, especially in places that you know are frequented by toughies.
- Project an air of confidence. This requires a bit of acting, but if you walk with your shoulders up, with

erect posture, and not slouched over, you can get by. Don't avert your eyes or quicken your pace if someone approaches you.

- Don't be attached to your possessions. If someone confronts you and forces you to relinquish your wallet, watch, new sneakers, or any other material object, give it and give it quickly. A possession is replaceable. Your life is not.

- Don't be afraid to tattle at times. Telling on someone may not usually be the noble thing to do, but sometimes someone's got to do it. Otherwise, a dangerous bully won't know that his or her behavior will not be tolerated. Advise your child to report one person's continued bullying to you and then decide together on the next step.

TEACHERS WHO ARE TERRIFYING

When you're young, teachers are scary because they seem to know everything and you know nothing. Later, when you're a teenager, teachers are scary because they seem to know nothing and you know everything. In either case, they're always scary because, whether you respect them or not, they seem to have the power to give you a good grade or a bad. Your future seems to be in their hands; they're in control.

At some point in your life as a student, however, there was hopefully at least one teacher you loved, one for whom you wanted to do your personal best. Similarly, there was at least one who appeared to have gotten a Ph.D. in Purgatory, a humorless ogre who loved to make you feel two inches tall in front of your peers, a disciplinarian with whom you had a major personality clash for the entire year—and your year-end grade proved it!

As I've said before, it helps you gain perspective on what your child is going through by recalling your own childhood experiences. You can assume that technological advances and thousand-channel cable access have not changed these basics of growing up.

Children will always have teachers they fear and those they love. Some of it is the luck of the draw. Explain this to your child. If there is a teacher known for being a tough disciplinarian, you can steel your child to the experience by reminding her to be on her best behavior in that teacher's class.

If your child breaks into a cold sweat when she even talks about walking into one certain loathed teacher's room, it may be time to interrogate her a little further. First, ask her exactly what it is about this teacher that frightens her. If it's that she's afraid of being called on when she hasn't done her homework, the solution is easy: Do your homework.

You can also talk to other parents and their children to find out if this dread is universal. If so, your youngster can draw some comfort in knowing that she's not alone. This may be the Teacher From Hell, the one who scares every class and who's considered a kind of rite of passage before graduation. "Just think," you can tell your child, "if you survive this teacher, you will become part of school history!"

You can also talk to the school administration and, without hurling your own epithets, inquire diplomatically as to whether this teacher perennially causes students concern. Perhaps the teacher has been going through his own personal hell since your child started his class, having lost a loved one or been diagnosed with some serious disease. Maybe the teacher is taking his own problems out on the students. In that case, the administration might not be aware that this is happening, and you'd be doing them a service.

There is another alternative, but it's one I have mixed feelings about. I'd suggest this only in cases with highly sensitive children who are having a very difficult time with a particular teacher. Sometimes too much is just too much to ask of your child. If so, you can ask for your child to be transferred to another class. This may, however, send your child a message that if there's some aspect of life he doesn't like, he can expect to be "transferred" out of having to deal with it. That message is sometimes appropriate, sometimes not; use your common sense on this one. If you can encourage your child to deal with a bad hand, you may be doing him or her a great service when that first boss in that great new job turns out to be an ogre.

HOMEWORK: HEAVEN OR HELL?

The social jungle aside, the real stress of school happens at home—as in homework. Children as young as seven suffer stress symptoms over homework and tests, some to the point where they consider suicide, according to a 1996 survey. This study found that mounting pressure to succeed has made academic work a top worry in children's lives. It pinpointed parental pressure, fears about the future, and children's lack of anyone to talk to about their worries.

Students spend on average about an hour and a half a night doing homework. Some can drag that out the whole night; others may never get to it. As parents, we know the benefits of encouraging our children to complete homework assignments. Frankly, only a small part of it has to do with mastering the subject at hand—though that shouldn't be minimized. But the greater lessons of tackling homework every night have to do with practicing concentration, organization, and self-control; defeating procrastination; and meeting deadlines.

But all of this may not be an enticing enough sales pitch to convince kids to turn off the tube, stop teasing their kid brother, put off e-mailing friends all over the world, and finally memorize the Pythagorean theorem. So here are some guidelines to get them into the homework frame of mind. The key is to create a regimen they can follow; though they may claim otherwise, kids love the regularity of things.

- Designate a work space. Help your kids find a place where they feel most comfortable doing homework. It could be at a desk in their bedroom—but it doesn't have to be. The kitchen table is fine if there isn't a lot of traffic and distraction there. I can safely say that in front of the TV is not a good place, though kids may adamantly claim it's the perfect spot. Whatever place they pick, help them arrange it as an optimal working environment—with adequate lighting, plenty of surface area, a comfortable (but not too) chair, drawers for pencils, shelves for dictionaries and other research books, slots and folder holders. Make that space theirs for homework; everyone in the family should know this and honor the sanctity of the homework space.
- Schedule homework time. Following the kids-love-routines philosophy, establish a time when homework is to be done. No "ifs," "ands," or "buts." It can be right after school, right after dinner, or right after their favorite TV show. Whatever it is, help them stick to it. Same time, same place, every night. If they say they have no homework, I suggest you encourage them to do "fun reading" of books that aren't necessarily on their syllabus just to get them to maintain the homework habit.
- Do the hard stuff first. Recommend to your youngster that tackling the hardest assignment first, the one that causes the most stress, means that once that one is over, the rest is all downhill. Their stress levels

will drop and they'll finish on a positive note—a note, by the way, that will motivate them to pick up the next night where they left off.

■ Monitor their progress. As a parent, your job is not to do the homework but to be there as a support system and to make sure that the assignment for the next day is finished. Make it part of the regimen for you to check over their work. That serves two purposes: one is to make sure they're doing it, and the other is make sure they're doing it right. If they're not finished at the specified time, find out what the problem is. Are they confused about the assignment? Or are they just not concentrating?

■ Don't pretend you know something you don't know. If a subject causes you more stress than it causes your child, you're hurting—not helping—the cause. You could turn homework into a negative experience if your child also has to deal with your stress. If your child needs help and you don't know the answers (or don't know how to find the answers), get an older student or a tutor to be a buffer. (Save the real stress for when you teach your child to drive.)

■ Shower praise on your children. Give them lots of positive reinforcement, more for their efforts than for their correct answers to homework questions. Mistakes will be made; that's to be expected. That's what homework is for. It's the process you're trying to get them comfortable with. Every once in a while—but not always—incentives and rewards are a nice treat for working through a tough homework assignment.

■ Let them control their environment. As long as the work gets done on time and is neat and accurate, don't worry that the room they're working in looks like a disaster area. Have you seen the desks of some CEOs or creative geniuses? And if your kids work well with the music on, that's their call too. As long as there are *no lyrics*, studies show, music can actually boost concentration. Be flexible—as long as the work gets done.

- Let them work in groups occasionally—again, as long as the work gets done well and on time. In fact, study clubs are a great way for children to draw motivation from their peers. Your child may find it lonely to study by herself every night; she may wonder if she's the only kid in the world stuck doing homework. Also, group problem solving will probably be a useful skill to bring to the workforce.

- Remember: all work and no play makes for a dull Debbie and a boring Bill. Not to mention the fact that playtime recharges the batteries worn down by doing too much homework. As much as you should let your child know you value learning, if you see him going overboard and starting to get burned out by the stress of it all, make a rare exception and break the routine by giving him a night off. Take him to a movie or someplace you never go on a weeknight. The next night you may be surprised to see how much he'll look forward to that homework. Well, you can hope.

Chapter 5

Family Stress

After school stress, the second most frequently mentioned cause of stress among children who responded to the KidStress Survey was family. Some of their comments are so poignant—and touch so many of the basic worries that children have about family—that I can think of no better way to start this chapter than to cite several. When asked "What kinds of things concern you?" here's what some wrote:

"Parents staying together."
"My mother dying and leaving me all alone."
"Disagreements with family."
"The safety of my family."
"We are in the Navy. We change places a lot . . . I hate my dad being out to sea."
"I miss my grandparents in Idaho. Most of all my family."
"If one of my family members will die or be injured seriously."

"My dad hitting me."

"I'm worried about family dying."

"My parents leaving me or dying."

"Abuse in my family; my sister stealing my things."

"My parents and money."

"When my family is out and has not returned home or called, I get worried."

"Will my parents get a divorce?"

"I worry about my family because some relatives are very sick."

"My dad's drinking."

"If my parents really want to keep me."

"Is my father ever going to see what my stepmother is doing to his relationship with his family, including his children?

These children are giving voice to fears they may never express out loud to anyone, especially not to their parents. In a way it's ironic. Relationships—and I'm speaking here of close relationships with people we care about, trust, and love—are a double-edged sword when it comes to stress. They can be both the cause of and the antidote to stress. In either case, we cannot escape the family into which we are born.

THE NEW BABY MEETS THE FAMILY

We know too well the stress placed on parents when, after those nine long, expectant months, baby has arrived. No one could have prepared you for those first nervous days and weeks when the slightest cough or the wrong sound coming from that vulnerable, helpless soul would send you into fits of anxiety. Slowly but surely, however, you became more confident as a parent.

Now consider stress from the baby's point of view. There she was, happily wrapped in this warm, moist blanket in a muffled and dark space, in suspended animation, a full supply of food at her disposal, no need for diaper changes. The perfect womb, without a view! Then, suddenly it seems, she moves into a harshly lit, cold and noisy world.

Between nervous new parents and an anxious new human being, you'd expect that stress levels would run high. But at least the parents had all that time to prepare. The baby has no prep time. She's thrown into the mix from the moment she is born. First there's that thing called breathing. Then there's the adjustment to all that intense light and those loud noises. Then comes another new sensation: hunger. And that's just for starters.

But mainly there's all these new people to get adjusted to. Meeting new people can trigger even an adult's stress response, especially when they're important people. How about the very first people you ever met in your life? Baby is already familiar with Mom—at least from the inside. Now she gets to meet her face-to-face. Instant recognition?

Then there's this other person, the one with the deep voice, scratchy face, and thick hands. "Hi, Dad. Now give me back to Mom, quick!"

And there may be this other entity (or two) in the family, a pint-sized version of the big people. This small person touches baby's face awkwardly, squeezes baby's hand a little too tightly, tugs on baby's nose and ears a little too vigorously, and (probably in frustration that baby is not responding appropriately and in anger that suddenly everyone is paying way too much attention to baby) pinches baby's arm until baby starts to cry. Say hi to your big sister or brother. And welcome to sibling stress.

These—along with the extended family of grandparents, aunts and uncles, and others—are the key players who nurture or annoy your child. Probably both. Let's look first at a child's siblings.

BIRTH ORDER

Through no fault of their own, babies born into families with brothers and sisters are immediately forced to deal with the stress of having siblings. Is birth order a real factor in what kind of personality the child will develop? The data say yes.

Let's start with *first-borns:*

- Statistics show that first-borns will eventually be more likely to excel on the Scholastic Aptitude Test, earn a Ph.D., and be listed in *Who's Who in America.*
- As one example of excellence, twenty-one out of the first twenty-three American astronauts were first-born or only children.
- And 50 percent of U.S. presidents have been first-borns.

Why? Probably because their parents are first-timers who tend to be very protective and very involved—a perfect recipe for raising children who may become approval junkies and workaholics. As University of Michigan social psychologist Hazel Markus has reported, "First-borns develop particular ideas and expectations about power, leadership, and responsibility; about what is socially acceptable and about the importance of friendships and relationships with other people. These ideas are likely to be markedly different from those that develop in later-borns."

So if you have more than one child, help the oldest fight her special stresses in the following ways:

1. Help her learn to limit the number of projects she takes on.

2. Don't set goals for her that were actually goals you never achieved for yourself.
3. Get her involved in play groups with peers early in life so that she can develop social skills before you have another baby.
4. Encourage her to share.
5. Set up situations for her in which she is not the leader but the follower.
6. Praise her for who she is, not what she's accomplished.
7. Let her know you love her even when she fails at something.
8. Praise her humor and generosity as much as her grades.
9. Encourage her to have fun!

Now for *second- and middle-born* children. Are they likely to feel less special than older or younger sibs?

- A National Institute of Mental Health study compared the parenting of three-month-old first-born and second-born siblings. It found that parents really did spend less time with their second-borns than with their first-borns in social, affectionate, and care-giving interactions.
- Stanford University psychologist Eleanor Maccoby and colleagues at the Stanford Longitudinal Project watched mother–child behaviors and found that mothers really were more protective of their first-borns than of their second-borns.
- University of Cincinnati students found in a study that later-borns are less likely to think that people hold them in high regard, and therefore their self-esteem rated lower.

In addition, later-borns find it difficult to assert their independence since they had not only parents but also older siblings to treat them as dependent and in need of help. Similarly, because parents' attention necessarily becomes more divided when a second child is born, that child may get less stimulation and encouragement to reach goals.

The reason parents are often less involved with their second-borns may also be that they are less anxious about their own skills as parents. After gaining confidence with the first child, they allow later-borns more freedom. The effect, however, is that later-borns often feel misunderstood or left out. They complain that they are constantly compared to the older children and that their accomplishments (first steps, first recital, first honor roll) are not acknowledged by parents with the same enthusiasm that the first-borns received.

The good news, however, is that studies suggest that later-borns appear to be less anxious and less controlling than first-borns, more likely to be team players, and more likely to value friends who care about them. And, according to a study by psychologists Norman Miller and Geoffrey Maruyama at the University of Southern California, later-borns seem to have greater popularity than first-borns. In this study, later-borns were more likely to be chosen as people to play with or sit by in class than were first-borns or only children. "They seldom have a direct pipeline to those in control of the family organization and must therefore learn to work with and around other family members to achieve their goals," says Hugh Markus.

In addition, from the start, the second-born has a live-in peer to interact with and so develops more social skills that serve him or her later in life. By the way, middle children also are the most likely to be monogamous and least likely to go into therapy!

Knowing all this, parents can try a couple of these suggestions to help middle children:

1. Listen—really listen—to them when they ask you questions or want to tell you about their day in school.
2. Ask their opinions and quote them in front of the rest of the family.
3. Don't set an older sibling up as the model to which they should conform.
4. Let them hear you praise them in front of other people.
5. Help them set goals for themselves, on their own terms, that still motivate them to live up to their potential.
6. Take lots of photographs of them at all ages. Middle children often complain that they feel left out of the family photo album.
7. Set aside special time with them alone—no brothers, no sisters, just them.

Last but not least, what about the *youngest* child? The last-born's biggest stress, say child-care experts, is always getting blamed by older siblings because the kids all know that their parents will spare the baby. And since parents are typically more tired and busier by the time their last is born, the youngest learns to fight for attention from his or her parents or older brothers and sisters. Last-borns also learn that they don't come first, say child psychologists. They learn to consider others' needs. Studies say they are even more likely to tolerate waiting in line. They learn to wait their turn. Here are some things to keep in mind with your youngest:

1. Since this one is the least likely to have a fair share of your attention, make it a point to spend time alone with her. And make it high-quality time.

2. Encourage the "baby" to do things by himself and not always be taken care of by his older sibs.

3. Like with child number two, let number three or four or five know she is heard and respected, too. Seek out her opinions on matters. Don't make light of her thoughts or feelings in front of the other children.

4. Find play groups for him with children his own age so he doesn't become used to playing only with older kids.

Now for the only child. Parents used to think children needed a sibling in order to grow up normal; therefore, being an only child was an exception in itself. Today there are about 13.5 million only children in the United States, and since many couples are waiting longer before starting families and are worrying more about money, we can expect increasing numbers of one-child families.

Let's look at some of the myths and realities about only children.

The stereotype is that only children are shy. The truth is that while they don't have much practice physically fighting with children near their age, a study of two hundred only children found that they're better at fighting verbally since, without sibs around, they've learned to fight with parents and other adults.

The stereotype says they're lonely. However, demographic studies find that only children tend to have more friends than children from large families because they're more motivated to do so; also, they usually develop a sibling-type relationship with at least one of them. My only-child daughter (remember that convergent-thinking trial lawyer I mentioned in chapter 3?) and her only-child best friend fought like sisters, shared like sisters, and remained as close as sisters for many years. Children usually seek out what they need. Only children are also likely to share well, since they have little practice in hoarding and hiding. They also assume leadership roles since they are used to making decisions.

The stereotype says they're neurotic. The truth is that five different studies have found that only children are less likely than first-borns or middle children to end up in therapy when they grow up, even when they are raised in a single-parent home. This is probably because they get a lot of undivided attention.

The stereotype says that only children are intellectual nerds. Well, yes and no. Only children do have all the high-achievement expectations and stresses of first-borns, but social adjustment scales say they're no more likely to be eccentric or nerdy than any other child.

The stress risk for only children is that they are less likely than other children to get sufficient playtime with their peers. They are often in the company of adults and, like oldest children, get undivided attention. That focus builds self-esteem, but it also increases stress. So . . .

1. Make sure your only child has downtime: playtime, silly time, just-for-fun time.
2. Build in time for roughhousing or some other jousting. Some good-natured joking and teasing are good ways for them to build defenses and practice for schoolyard play.
3. Make sure their stresses are children's stresses—not adult stresses, not your stresses.
4. Raise a child, not a friend. Your only child is not your companion, not your protégé, not your confidant. Remember that you are an adult and your child

is a child. Parents—especially single parents—tend to forget this and burden their children with grown-up stresses they can't handle.

THE STRESS OF SIBLING RIVALRY

We asked children to finish two sentences that would provide us insight into their relationships with their siblings. First, the downside. When asked to tell us the *worst part* of having a brother or sister, their responses echoed universal complaints about sibs:

"My brothers mess with my stuff."
"My sisters annoy me."
"My brother hits me."
"My sister intentionally tries to hurt my feelings."
"My brother instigates [trouble with] me."
"My brother takes my stuffed animals and hangs them on the fan."
"I get in trouble for doing what my little sister does, and . . . she bugs me, by following me around."
"My sister acts like a brat."
"My little sister fakes being sick so she can quit playing a game."
"My sister takes my stuff without asking me first."
"I have to miss out on doing stuff because I have to take care of my brother."
"My sister doesn't let me watch the show I want to."
"My older brother calls me fat."

However, we heard a different story when we asked the *best part*. The answer we heard most frequently was "having someone to play with." But as I mentioned in chapter 2, speaking of having "someone around who knows how I feel sometimes," someone who will "watch out for you, and stick up for you," and "a good friend forever," they also showed signs of appreciation, of honoring an intimacy and a protectiveness that gives all parents hope.

Sibling rivalry happens. Recall that children rank fighting with a sibling as one of the most frequent behavioral stress symptoms; 60 percent said so. There's no avoiding it. It's as natural as, well, stress. And it can happen in biblical proportions—remember Cain and Abel? Only four chapters into the Old Testament and we have society's first murder: fratricide. Cain slew Abel out of jealousy at their father's preference for Abel.

Sibling rivalry happens when children vie with each other for the love of their parents. That old bit the Smothers Brothers comedy team used to do was funny because they hit it on the nail: a seemingly dense but sensitive Dicky would lament to his self-confident brother Tommy, "Mom always loved you more."

The rivalry can leave children with some lifelong scars or at least a lifelong question of where they fit into a family or a community. Your children will often identify themselves in their peer groups as they did among their siblings, and as you cast them: the funny one, the jock, the genius, the peacemaker, the troublemaker, and so on.

And though the rivalry between sibs may subside—as a result of maturity, success in the world, the healing effect of time, and the probable effect of distance—embers of that competitive fire between and among brothers and sisters may still flicker.

In a paper presented to the American Psychological Association several years ago, University of Cincinnati psychologists Helgola Ross and Joel Milgram made a strong case for the persistence of sibling rivalry into adulthood. Of sixty-five sub-jects ages twenty-five to ninety-three, 71 percent said they had been rivalrous with a brother or sister. Of those, 36 percent claimed to have overcome the feelings, but 45 percent admitted that the feelings were still alive. Half said the rivalrous attitudes were precipitated by parents favoring one sibling over another. And, they added, when competition continued into adulthood, it was fueled by the continuation of parental favoritism.

In times of greater stress, those dying embers can easily be sparked into raging conflagrations. Although Purdue University developmental psychologist Victor Cicirelli found in a twelve-year study of sibling relationships that siblings remain important to each other into old age, sometimes becoming more important with time, he also discovered that siblings' negative feelings toward each other surface during that stressful period when their parents become more dependent or seriously ill. Typically, the younger will expect the older to take care of the parent, while the older will resent the younger for shirking the responsibility. Conversely, some sibs compete to do the most for the dependent parent, with the younger or less-favored child viewing the parent's need of help as an opportunity to win a lifelong family contest. Finally, after the death of a parent, sibs may jockey for leadership positions as they move into the roles of family elders.

One problem psychologists identified as contributing to the difficulty of sorting out these rivalries—even into adulthood—was that most siblings rarely talked about their rivalry. Successful siblings often did not even know their achievements were causing envy, and siblings who felt inferior did not want to say so. As Ross and Milgram stated, "Admitting sibling rivalry may be experienced as equivalent to admitting maladjustment. To reveal feelings of rivalry to a brother or sister who is perceived as having the upper hand increases one's vulnerability in an already unsafe situation."

With brothers relating to brothers, this problem is made worse by the fact that men are not as well trained in verbal communication as women are. Bert Adams says, in his book *Kinship in an Urban Setting*, that grown men report less closeness and contact with brothers than women do with sisters, even when differences of geographical closeness are taken into account.

But societal changes are making reconciliation between brothers and sisters more important than ever before. As Michael Kahn points out in his book *The Sibling Bond*, "siblings are becoming more and more dependent upon one another in contemporary families because of the attrition in family size. If you have only one sibling, that one becomes enormously important." Divorce, one-parent homes, two working parents, and the geographical split-up of nuclear families all underscore the need for siblings to maintain contact with one another.

Here are some other things to keep in mind that will help *you* cope with the stress of sibling rivalry:

- The amount of conflict between children is not necessarily related to their affection for each other, according to research conducted by psychologist Wyndol Furman at the University of Denver. Some name-calling among siblings should not be as much of a concern as aggressive acts toward other kids outside the family.

- Sibling rivalry can be a good training ground for important skills children will need as they grow. Specifically, conflict between siblings can help children learn and practice conflict-resolution skills, suggests psychologist Frances Fuchs Schacter. And it's a relatively safe training ground. They can take risks because a brother or sister will not usually reject them the way friends might.

- Squabbles help siblings establish that they're different from each other, which is why fights are most intense between siblings who are of the same sex and close in age.

- Fighting is also a way for siblings to release frustration at an adult—or displaced anger toward a parent—whom they wouldn't dare insult or torment the way they would a sibling.

- Fighting may worsen when an older child moves up to the next age group—like from junior high to high school. It's a way for older kids to distance themselves from the younger group they've just left, which a kid sister reminds them of.

- Siblings who feel they're being treated unequally or unfairly by their parents may start a fight to determine which one of them a parent favors. You can tell this is the case when the fighting ends as soon as you leave the room or stop paying attention.

- Appearances deceive. Vicious fights may appear devastating, but they may consist of more smoke than fire. Some of that screaming may be intended to get your attention. Again, if you leave the room and the bickering subsides, that's a sure sign that the siblings are fighting for your benefit.

- More good news: the intense rivalry between sibs will often disappear when they reach adolescence. Increased empathy makes them less likely to bully someone smaller. But beware: teenage siblings also learn to team up against parents.

- Encourage your children to talk over their differences, but not in the middle of a major conflict. Instead, during periods when they are feeling close, suggest that they name the things they like about each other. Then ask them to list the things they'd like to change about each other. Facilitate—but don't lead—the discussion. When this works, it really works!

CHILDREN COPING WITH THE STRESS OF DIVORCE

While children told us they worried about money troubles, a parent's drinking problem, physical abuse, or simply whether a parent would be there for them, it was the cloud of divorce that most concerned children. Of the children who responded to the children's KidStress Survey, 20 percent said their parents were divorced, and 12 percent said they were dealing with a parent's second spouse. But I sensed from many responses that a great percentage of children are acutely aware of those 20 percent whose parents are divorced.

If change causes stress, then it stands to reason that divorce should rank among the top three potential stressors in a child's life, right up there with moving and the death of a parent. In fact, divorce is like a death—if not of one or the other parent, then of a separate entity the child had come to think of as Mommy/Daddy. The loss of that institution and the shelter it represented—and the change in schedules, the emotional shift, and the physical adjustment to the new environment of the parent who moves out as well as to the new feel of home—all spell stress for a child at any age.

One saving grace is that, with the divorce rate still hovering at 50 percent, your children will not be alone in dealing with this. Close to half the kids at their school are children of divorce. Reminding them of this may ease their stress just a bit; at least they won't feel like aliens from some foreign planet. They (and you) may also want to talk to some of the parents and their children who have been through it already. You'll both see that there is quite often a happy ending.

To make sure that the stress of divorce does not destroy a child's life, use the utmost consciousness and consideration when you're dealing with to both your child and—as hard as this may be—your ex-spouse. It can help your child survive the breakup and emerge as an emotionally and physically healthy young adult. Children of divorce do not necessarily suffer life-long stress scars that blemish their self-view and their outlook on the intimate relationships they'll enter into throughout their own lives.

Surviving the Breakup, based on a long-term study of the effects of divorce on children, and in her follow-up to that study, *Second Chances*, psychologist Judith Wallerstein agrees that children can indeed survive the dissolution of the marriage of their biological parents. But it's not easy.

BREAKING UP IS HARD TO DO

One of the most stressful aspects of divorce for children relates to that basic issue that contributes so much to stress in general: loss of control. Here's a situation in which a lot of what has contributed to the unraveling of a marriage has gone on behind closed doors, after the child has gone to bed, or perhaps before the child was even born. Older children may be cognizant of disharmony—they hear the fights, feel the tension in the air, witness the lack of caring and affection between their parents—but they still don't know why it exists. Other events at play between the parents are not just out of sight but out of the child's control. Divorce leaves children feeling powerless;

they may feel like they're free-falling off a steep cliff with no net below them, no sight of the ground below, and no sense of how long they're going to keep falling. In many cases, they may feel it's their fault. Ironically, this may be one way in which they think they can gain back control; that is, they may think there's something they can do to save the marriage and thus control the situation. Sadly, their attempts are futile.

I'd like to suggest that you become as aware as humanly possible that every argument, every dagger-glance between you and your spouse that your child witnesses, will cause stress waves through his or her little body. In the midst of those early days during the breakup of your marriage, it may go against the intense current of emotions racing through you, but if it's possible to hold your tongue or save that angry stare until you and your soon-to-be ex are both out of sight or hearing of your youngsters, you'll be saving them from stressors not of their own making. If you haven't already sought professional counseling, do so—this time not to see how to mend the relationship with your estranged partner but how to minimize the traumatic effect of divorce on your child. Years later, when the dust of divorce has settled and hopefully all of you have found a way to cope with the permanent rupture of the original family unit without too much residual acrimony, your child may thank you.

THE SINGLE-PARENT HOME

Many men and women in bad, unloving, and sometimes even downright destructive relationships try to stay together "for the sake of the kids," as they so selflessly put it. And sometimes they *are* being selfless. But sometimes it's simply a rationale from an adult who is too afraid to deal with the stress of being single and alone again. Or it could be that the adult is assuming that growing up in a single-parent home will be a very stressful experience for the children.

What does the research show? Does it make a difference whether a child is brought up by one parent or two? Some answers, based on data provided by children's own bodies, were offered by researchers at the University of Missouri. Over a five-year period, they studied how much of the stress hormone cortisol was produced by close to 250 children living in the Caribbean island of Dominica in a variety of domestic situations. Twice a day the researchers took a saliva sample and asked the children how they felt and what they'd been doing. Predictably, perhaps, children with the lowest stress levels had both parents living together. But even when Dad was away half the time, cortisol levels were the same. In fact, the results were the same for children living with grandparents or with single moms living with relatives.

Children living with single mothers on their own, however, had stress levels significantly higher than others, and about the same as children living with a lone father. The highest stress levels were reported among children living with their mother and a stepfather and the stepfather's children from a previous marriage. Living with distant relatives was cause for equally high stress.

This study also showed that stress within the family could cause cortisol levels to remain elevated for several days—very different than, say, the peak in cortisol after a game of football or some other exciting experience. Another interesting fact, based on gender, came out of this research. In families that had had a lot of stress since the children were infants, because either the mother was often away or there was extreme conflict within the family, the boys had unusually low cortisol levels much of the time except for the occasional peak linked with fighting or delinquent behavior. Under the same conditions however, girls were more likely to have high cortisol levels most of the time and to be anxious and withdrawn. This may be due to the gender conditioning we examined in chapter 3. Boys are trained from an early age not to show their emotions—until, finally, the feelings become so powerful that they explode, sometimes violently. Meanwhile, girls are encouraged and expected to be constantly in touch with their emotions, even the "bad" ones.

A Canadian study backed up the idea that children being raised by single mothers often undergo higher levels of stress than children in other family arrangements. They face increased risks of emotional, behavioral, academic, and social problems, according to the eight-month study. In Canada, it was found, one in six children lives in a family headed only by a woman. On average those families were far poorer than two-parent families. But the study found that the incidence of stress problems was high even among children of well-off single moms—even higher than among children from poor two-parent families. The problem, the researchers concluded, could therefore not be attributed to financial difficulties alone but rather to the tough job of juggling all the responsibilities of home and work. Somewhere, somehow, something or someone has got to give: most likely it's the children who pay with their own stress for Mom's stressed-out life.

This does not mean that single moms are bad mothers or that raising a child on your own will automatically produce a great deal of stress in that child's life. But it will be extra difficult due to circumstances often beyond your control. If you need to find a smaller apartment to make ends meet, for example, your child will have to change not only homes but probably schools and friends as well. That's stressful. Knowing this, a single parent can make all the changes less stressful simply by talking about them. You can work together on planning steps and strategies for sharing some of the responsibilities. I said sharing, not completely off-loading those responsibilities to a child ill prepared to, say, raise a young sibling. But making your children feel part of the process, as opposed to part of the problem, may teach them also that they can cope with change. And it will make them stronger individuals, more able to deal with the stressors life throws at them.

JOINT CUSTODY

Though you may have split up with your husband or wife, your child has not. And probably did not want to, even if she saw how bad the marriage was. Children want and need to spend time with and have access to both their parents, even if those parents never want see each other again. I told you this wasn't going to be easy.

How well you and your ex work at making joint custody as cooperative an effort as possible will reduce some of the stress of adjustment for your children. It will also reduce stress for you. And, unless you want every single changing of the guard between you and your ex to be full of anxiety, you'd better find a way to ease that tension—because, until your child graduates from college or goes out on her own entirely, the irony of divorce is that, if there are children involved, the other partner will continue to be in your life. At some point, maybe you will have pushed through your differences and can go as a team to your children's recitals or games, or even work together on planning the graduation or wedding.

Here are some other guidelines:

- Keep the transitions between households smooth and regular. This is particularly true during the first two years after divorce. Establish as reliable a schedule as possible so that your child knows, for example, that Tuesday, Wednesday, and Thursday he's at Mom's and Friday, Saturday, Sunday, and Monday he's at Dad's. Or that he alternates one week with Mom, one with Dad.

- Explain changes of plans. If the schedule has to change, discuss it with your children as soon as you know. Explain why the schedule needs to be disrupted and, hopefully, when it will return to normal. To the extent that it's possible, involve them in making a plan B.

- Show respect for your ex in front of your children. Say thank you and show other forms of courtesy as you would to any friend or acquaintance. (Talk to your ex privately about this so that you each understand the importance of it—even if you don't mean it.) Apologize for lateness; better yet, don't be late since continued lateness can sometimes be seen as a passive form of aggression.

- Don't argue in front of each other as though the children are not there. When divorced people are polite, studies show, children say they feel less trapped in the middle, less guilty about still loving both parents, less like the wishbone being pulled from each end.

Even if staying together for the sake of the kids didn't seem like such a great idea when you were married, working together after you've split up for the sake of the kids *is* a great idea if your children's emotional and physical well-being are truly your concern. So, difficult as it may be at times, give it a try—for the kids.

Meanwhile, if it just seems like more than you can handle, I encourage you to talk to a mental health professional—a counselor, therapist, or psychologist. That's how important this is.

Because the research—mine and that of others—is clear: the less conflict there is in joint parenting, the better children do in school and with their friends, and the better they will adapt to the changes that divorce brings to their lives.

THE NEW PERSON IN YOUR LIFE: DATING AND OTHER RAMIFICATIONS OF BEING A SINGLE PARENT

You've gotten over the breakup, and so have your children. Now, because you are a human being with a heart that has begun to open again, you meet someone new. Perhaps this was what you prayed for after the end of your marriage. You even convinced yourself—and maybe even your children too—that a better partner would be good for you and for them. A new mate would add emotional, maybe also financial, stability. It would reconstruct the nuclear family that had been blasted apart. It would be an opposite-sex role model—not, you assured your kids, to replace the father or mother they don't see as frequently as they did before but just someone who could be there for them.

But you hadn't really looked at it from your child's point of view. To your youngster, this person with whom you feel closeness is a stranger, an intruder, an interloper. And there is so much to worry about as a child: What if I start to like this person—and then he (or she) goes away? Will this person like me—or vice versa? Will this new person be mean to Mommy (or Daddy)—or, equally as bad, get all her (or his) attention? Or will he (or she) simply just never seem like part of the family, never as good as Daddy (or Mommy)? These are the things that stress out your child even the first time you bring a new date into your home.

No one has written the rule book on this yet. Anyone who

has been through divorce can take some solace in knowing that this is largely uncharted territory. So here are some suggestions to help you and your child cross this new terrain:

- Start by asking your child how he feels about your dating. You may be worrying a lot more than you need to about how much *he* may be worrying about it. Even if he says he is worried, you shouldn't necessarily take some kind of monastic vow and stay home alone the rest of your life. You're soliciting his opinion first to validate that he does have feelings about it. Second, you're inviting a dialogue so that you can get information to help you steer him toward being more comfortable with the idea of your going out with someone new.

- Don't ask her advice about dating. That would be crossing the line from parent/child to parent/confidant. You don't need to ask your child's approval of your dates or your sex life. If you do involve your child in such a conversation, she's going to start feeling disloyal to the other parent and then guilty. Then she'll feel double guilt if she dislikes the person you're getting involved with.

- Keep your private life private, for a while. Having someone you've only just begun to date over to spend the night and wake up in the morning to a houseful of kids is not such a good idea—for all parties involved. Unless your date has spent time with your kids, made friends with them, and earned their trust, I'd discourage overnights altogether.

- Once a relationship is on firmer ground, prepare your children ahead of time if you decide it's right for you to invite someone to sleep over. Reassure your children that you're not abandoning them, that they are still your first priority. You can demonstrate this by maintaining bedtime and other rituals like meals. And tell them that their other parent is still their other parent, that they don't have to stop loving that other parent and start loving this new person.

■ I'd also think about offering your children a small dose of relationship reality by suggesting that just because you will be spending time with a new person, there's always the possibility this person will not become a lifelong mate. They may become a lifelong friend, instead, or a friend for a while. Try to make it the positive learning experience that meeting someone new can offer.

You might as well be reading this section aloud into a mirror because I'm sure you've already given yourself the same pep talk. But it doesn't hurt to remind yourself that it's fair and honest to let an older child know that bringing a new person into your life is both exhilarating and scary. Knowing that it will be difficult for you as well will free your child from thinking he is the only one struggling with this transition. But, as with all of life's other stressors, your child will take his cues from how well you handle this new phase in your lives.

STEPPARENTS

It started as a date, became serious, and now you've tied the knot. Your child, whether she likes it or not, has a new member of the family: a stepparent. Thanks to some bad stereotypes, children's fables, and other myths, the word alone evokes images of a mean old man or woman. The disciplinarian stepmother.

The loud-talking stepfather. Or worse: the neglectful or sexually abusive stepparent.

Stepparenting not easy for adults either. You fell in love with the man; his kids came along with the package. Now you're waking up in the morning to instant supermotherhood.

Or, Dad, if your new wife came to live with you and your kids, your children are waking up to a stranger in their house—an instant second parent. Here's someone threatening to break into the family circle, a circle your child now feels is both more precious and more tenuous than ever. As parents, we have to honor what that must feel like. And as our children's stress educators, our first step should be to give them the time, place, and space to express those fears and anxieties. They are, after all, highly justified. To diminish them or make light of them is unfair.

The second step—if not the first—should be to discuss your concerns with your new significant other. He or she needs to know that this is very difficult for your children. The new mate needs to know that your children are not going to automatically shift their allegiance from their biological parent to their stepparent.

As for your children, they'll probably let you know how much having a new stepparent stresses them in lots of ways, but very few will express that stress verbally—unless you count shouting and talking back to you. They will act out their stress by letting their grades drop or cutting classes. They may get sick more often. They may start hanging out with new friends they know you won't approve of, or playing music they know you disdain at intolerable decibel levels. They'll bleach their hair, find new and exotic body parts to pierce or tattoo, or wear clothes even they secretly think are unflattering. Or, depending on their age, they'll do all of the above with double doses of attitude thrown in for bad measure. Or they will give you the stone-cold silent treatment, retreating into their own wishful world where servants ply them with free ice cream all day and parents stay together forever.

Somehow you've got to figure out how to get them to open up and let it out. Don't try right after a tense blowup that may or may not have been sparked by an issue related to the stepparent. Wait for a moment when you both are in a good mood, feeling connected to each other and free of life's other stressors. Hopefully, you can direct the conversation from complaints and anger to acceptance of the situation. You should repeat as often as possible: I understand but this is the way it's going to be. Despite your efforts, however, some children will hang on to reunion fantasies for years.

Listen carefully to what bothers your child most about living with the stepparent. Watch for cues in your child's language that suggest a stubbornness or unwillingness to change and accept: "She always . . ." or "He never . . ." Very few people "always" or "never" do anything. Those are words of defiance, walls that people use to convince themselves of their point of view. If you hear about behaviors the stepparent can easily change or desist from, share that privately with your mate and see if he or she can take the higher road and make some changes and concessions.

If there are things your child is doing that only exacerbate the situation, such as purposefully persisting in a behavior that annoys your new spouse, patiently explain to your child that this helps no one, least of all the child herself.

Emphasize cooperation: life is a little give, a little take. Stress that all new situations are awkward. Ask your child what your new spouse can do to make it easier. But be firm about things that cannot change. All through the early adjustment, continue with rituals and schedules that comfort your child. But you be the one to put him to bed, or read to him. Don't delegate this to your new husband for quite a while. In the best of all possible worlds, late one night your child will ask if his stepfather can bring him a glass of water. In such small moments, great progress can be measured.

Don't take the bait and get into defending your new spouse. The last thing you want is to be stuck in the middle any more than you already are. With that in mind, after a series of talks with your child, suggest that your child and your spouse have a talk about the things each can do to make life together work better. If you're part of this meeting, you should downplay your role, perhaps only introducing the subject and the goal: to find mutually beneficial ways to learn to live together. Then step back, letting them talk and work it through. If you have to, bite your tongue, but remain patient and let them keep working it out. If things break down into shouting and incrimination, suggest that each go away and take a twenty-minute walk separately but agree to come back and continue the discussion right after the walk.

WHEN MOVING IN MEANS MOVING AWAY

Whether you move to your new spouse's house or vice versa, your child is going to feel displaced. Moving to another house will surely be the more disruptive move. But even if your new spouse moves in with you (and especially if he or she has children too), your child will have to give up some precious space. The playroom, the bathroom, the kitchen, the backyard, the back seat of the car—all will become common ground, without much in common with your child, in her view. Even if there aren't other children involved, it's still going to mean sharing— sharing you!

Let's look first at when the new husband or wife moves in with you and your children. This can go in two directions. It can be a great lesson in sharing, cooperation, altruism, and generosity. Or it can turn into an ugly struggle for power, for control of the turf, and control of you. It can open a child's heart, or close it.

Of course, I'm opting that you encourage the former. How? By being a good role model. Don't forget, you're going to go through a similar shift as well. You're going to have to relinquish some control of the kitchen, the bathroom, the living room, and your free time. How well you cooperate with your new mate can show your child the way as well—especially if you show concessions in areas your child knows are very important to you. Naturally, you'll need the complicity of your mate. You'll both have to model generosity, compromise, and understanding.

At the same time, it's important to allow your child certain areas, certain times, certain privileges that are uniquely her own: a corner of her world where no one else can go, a sanctum sanctorum that everyone else must respect, a responsibility that only she can handle. This will remind your child of her very special place in the world and in your world.

Moving into someone else's space will, of course, be much more difficult, if only because you'll simply have less control over the environment. Just thinking about packing will probably cause your heart to pound with anxiety. Even before you plow into the new house, it might be nice to honor the place you're leaving—and to show your children that memories are things you can take with you wherever you go—by taking pictures of the house or apartment and everyone's rooms and favorite places. You're creating family history. There are, hopefully, good memories attached to this place, as well as some difficult memories to get over.

During packing, help your kids pack their own things, so they feel some ownership in the process. At the other end, when their stuff is unpacked, they'll more likely experience a life-enlarging sense of continuity—not the sadness of endings and the scariness of beginnings. Before you vacate the house, think about bringing your own immediate family—you and your own children—together for one final farewell ritual. Perhaps stand in the empty bedroom that was theirs and recall with fondness and strength how much they learned and discovered about life, about themselves, about others, right here. And remind them again that all those memories, all those experiences—some good, some bad, all educational—come with you.

Resettling into your new spouse's home will require great patience and understanding on your and your partner's part. Don't forget that moving is near the top of everyone's "worst stressors" list. Your children will be thrown into a whole new environment, with new rules, new stuff to figure out ("How does this VCR work!"), not to mention new people to meet, a new school, new streets. An endless number of stressors can ruin a day in a new place, especially when none of this was of your own doing, as your children must feel.

Setting up a schedule that's familiar to your kids as quickly as possible will help. So will establishing new rituals. Help your child set up his new room or area. Find out whether he's leaning toward making it just like the room he left behind or interested in making a bold new personal statement. It's his choice; honor it as much as you can. Once again, having a long private conversation with your new spouse will ease the transition. He or she must remember who the adult is, and that there will have to be lots of accommodations made for a child being put through this traumatic adjustment.

In terms of the interpersonal relationship between your children and your new spouse, it's critical that all parties keep talking things through. As discussed, you can be the facilitator, but, as much as possible, let your children and spouse communicate directly with each other. One of the reasons to keep talking is that, as your children grow, the issues will change.

This is not a static relationship. Some issues will become moot, but others will surface.

Issues involving disciplinary actions, helping with homework, sharing hobbies, and even the degree to which the new parent can play a mentoring role may have to be approached delicately. Keep feeling out the child. Watch for those nonverbal clues I've been pointing out throughout this book. Slowly, though, I believe that, over time, a child will adjust to this new relationship.

If your ex is still in the picture and is an active and involved parent, your new spouse needs to appreciate and respect that fact. Your children will resent it if he or she tries to take over the other parent's role. And the harder he or she tries to be a "real" parent, the more resistance your child will put up. If taking the kids to Yankee games has been a favorite thing for your children to do with their father, then your new husband probably shouldn't do the same thing right away—even if he's a diehard Yankee fan.

THE NEW BROTHER AND SISTER

TV sitcoms aside, the blending of two whole families—kids, pets, special diets, toys, teen telephone lines—is usually no laughing matter. Your child did not bargain for the breakup of the nuclear family, did not necessarily look forward to your meeting and falling in love with someone new, and certainly did not count on having any more brothers and sisters than she already is tolerating.

But now there's this new kid (or kids) not just on the block but in the house and you're asking your children to treat these complete strangers like brothers and sisters. It's a lot to ask. Maybe you shouldn't ask—or expect—so much.

By the time you've tied the knot, your and your new mate's children should have had numerous chances to spend time with each other. I definitely would recommend it. I'd suggest casual get-togethers at first, not a formal dinner at a restaurant. Perhaps you can plan a movie picnic or activity that the kids can do together. Afterward, start a discussion about what you saw. Maybe you can even plan to watch one of those TV shows with the blended, extended families living together and then talk about how close to the truth it seemed (or didn't!). Once the ice has begun to melt, and before you all move in together, sit down with both sets of children and talk about the logistics of living together.

A good ear will be useful here. Listen, and listen carefully, to what's stressing them. Repeat what you hear so they know you are listening and understand. Also, acknowledge—out loud, to your children—that you sympathize, even empathize (inasmuch as you're going through it too) with their stress.

The nomenclature doesn't help the cause of brotherly love. "Half" or "step" before sister or brother seems to legitimize the feeling that this will never be a "whole" or real sibling. But that's okay. It's fine to simply encourage your child to first see the other set of kids as new friends. As such, of course, you'd be encouraging the same sort of behaviors—respect for others, respect for differences of opinion, cooperation, compromise, and other signs of courtesy—that you'd expect of your child in any friendship. (For more on the subject of friendships, see chapter 6.) However, this is a friendship that they won't be able to leave at the playground. It's a relationship that will have ramifications for your household and for your new marriage, and that will continue requiring differences to be worked out.

On the positive side, some children love the idea of gaining a sibling. Maybe they're not so thrilled with the ones they were born with. Your only son may be excited about having an older brother. Maybe your daughter is just as excited about having that same new older brother who's got all those cute guy friends.

Loving a stepfamily is not something you'll be able to force on your child. But like the other changes you've asked your child to endure, time, patience, and good role modeling will help him welcome these new people to his expanding definition of family.

CHAPTER 6

De-Stressing Friendships

Parents predicted that the greatest source of stress for children would be peer pressure: schoolyard bullies, best friends and fickle friends, groups and gangs. In fact, about 60 percent said "not being liked by friends" and 57 percent said "being teased" would cause anxiety for their children.

Parents may have been wrong about how their children would rank peer pressure (it ended third on the list), but they were right about the causes of peer stress. As I said in chapter 2, maybe parents understand peer pressure because our own memories of its stress are so vivid. Maybe, because family life was a bit more stable back then and intense competitiveness had not yet pervaded the school experience, our world of peer friendships was, by default, our top concern. Today, however, because of shifts in society, youth recognize that their best support system often comes from their age group. Those friendships, however, are still filled with their own stresses. Here, I repeat from chapter 3, is a sampling of kids' peer concerns:

"Having enough friends."

"Picking the wrong kinds of friends."

"I'm afraid that my friends will have better stuff than me."

"If people are going to say something mean to or about me."

"I worry about my friends a lot but especially about school, like if my clothes are okay and why the popular kids are so mean all the time and never accept me even though I am nice and funny."

"Friends who get messed up with the wrong people, so many crimes and stuff."

"My friends using drugs. I feel like I am losing them."

"When kids push people around and take a thing from a kid."

"Fights with friends."

"The way people think of me at school."

"If boys like me, if people like me."

"If friends would make fun of me."

"Wondering if my girlfriend will dump me."

"Friends going behind my back to other people."

"Social pressure, and sex!!! (I want it.)"

"Sexual orientation."

"My friends might turn their backs on me or make fun of me."

"Bullies."

"My friends hearing lies about me."

Some of the above—fears of bullies, of not being accepted, of trusting others—sound like things that have worried children about friendship since the beginning of time. Other concerns reflect the more recent increases in crime, drug use, and the complexity of questions about sexuality. But it's clear: though not at the top of every child's list, peer relationships certainly cause stress for many, many children.

When children are stressed by other children, expect a double dose of stress and its symptoms. Not only will they feel the effects of peer pressure, but they will also be deprived of one of their most potent stress-relievers: peer support. Friends can be a buffer against loneliness, depression, and stress. They can distract a worried child with games and jokes, with quips and that rapid-fire conversational style that requires their full attention. Friends may understand each other's world better than adults do, and can lend a more sympathetic ear. When your child has trouble with friends, you can try the following:

- When one friend disappoints, encourage your child to not give up in all friendships.
- Remind your child that to have a friend you have to be a friend, that when you give friendship you get it back.
- Remember that kids watch, study, and mimic us in our own friendships for clues about how to conduct theirs.
- Watch for how your child takes cues from the media—television, films, books, and magazines.

But perhaps children's strongest role models will be their own peer groups. That's why it's important to be especially attentive in their early years when their natural capacity for friendship is developing. What they learn then about how friendship can help them cope with stress will be remembered and valued well into adulthood.

AGES AND STAGES OF FRIENDSHIP

Put two-year-olds together and let them play with a roomful of toys and more than likely you'll see a few of them getting along very nicely—sharing, helping, cooperating. But there will probably be a larger number fighting for control of the toys, pulling things away from each other, crying, "Mine, mine!" At two, children have not learned to share. They are still in the midst of distinguishing between themselves and others. In their view, it's *all* theirs. The world revolves around them. So of course the toys are theirs. But slowly they learn the difference between "mine" and "yours," and by kindergarten-age they usually have it down pat.

As early as the third grade, children start learning the "mechanics of popularity," as University of Colorado sociologists Patti and Peter Adler put it. After interviewing some two hundred elementary school children, they found that kids work to master the predatory "pecking order" of preadolescent cliques. These cliques are formed through a complex social sorting process that would scare even the young people from *Beverly Hills 90210.*

"Kids really smell out fear and weakness and they use it," wrote Patti Adler. "They feed on it to strengthen themselves and they prey on the weak." Teasing and shunning are among the social weapons used in these clique cultures. They gradually form out of first- and second-grade friendship circles. By third grade they become exclusive. Then the rumor mill takes over, and members of the clique test the allegiance of others. Cliques are forms of bullying, one way a small society can arbitrarily determine who is in and who is out. Clothing, looks, ethnicity, and cultural background can all be the determinants of "in" or "out." This is how some children build their own tenuous self-esteem.

In chapter 4, we talked about how to help your child deal with bullies. What I want to add here draws on what I see happening with bullies but also applies to all children's peer relationships. It's a concept parents may have an easier time understanding than children, but if you can explain it to your child you will help her overcome friendship stress. Basically it's this:

> Everything people say and do
> is information about them, not you.

In other words, if someone makes fun of how smart you are, it tells you that *he* feels insecure about his own intelligence. If someone calls you a loser, she's worried people will think that of *her*. If he works to ostracize you from some exclusive clique, you can bet *his* biggest fear is to be left out too.

Of course, before your youngster jumps to the conclusion that she is completely innocent, she should ask herself whether she did anything to provoke an attack. If not, then she should ask herself what may be going on with the other child. Is that child making fun of your child's parents because her own are splitting up? Is she dropping your child as a friend because she was dropped by someone else? Is this the type of person who changes friends as frequently as she changes sweaters?

Part of what you're teaching your child is empathy. You're asking your child to put herself in the other kid's place rather than remain focused on looking at the world only through her own eyes. You're also helping her become a good judge of character. Who is worth her time and emotional energy? Who is not?

I said this may be a hard concept to get across, not because it's that complicated—it's really basic human nature—but because children are able to grasp the idea only when they are mature enough. That age varies from child to child. It's pointless to try to pound this notion into a child until he's reached that age. You can't punish it into him, nor can you do to him the same thing the other child did. Ignoring your child to demonstrate what it would feel like to be ignored will only teach him the fine points of how to withhold attention and friendship. It would be better to model positive behavior. Point to your own friendships, for example. It's not what you say that will make a difference; it's what they see you doing.

Similarly, you may not know when your child is going through turmoil with his peers by what he says; he may say nothing. But you'll learn by studying his behavior. If he's suddenly asking you to drive him to school rather than take the bus, it may be because there's someone on the bus who is bothering him. If he's spending time in his room on nice days when you know he usually is outside with his friends, it's possible his friends are causing him grief. If he tells you he's sick when his friends invite him to go bowling, and you know he's not sick at all, be concerned.

The need for friends seems to be natural; the ability to make and keep friends is often not. But it is something you can learn. Much of the skill you learn by hit or miss, but parents can help. Encourage him to invite other children to do things with him, and to accept invitations when they are extended. Friendships are a microcosm in which your child learns about the fulfillment of giving and caring. When a friend is sick, suggest that your child send a note or bring over some chicken soup. It's usually at birthdays that children exchange gifts, but it might be nice to let friends know how much you like them at any time.

On the other side of the friendship coin, confronting someone who has hurt or disappointed her can cause a child stress. As an adult, you know it's not easy. We need to show our children that caring about someone also means that it's okay to tell that person how we feel when she has said something that offended us. It's okay to tell someone that being very late or not showing up for an appointment makes you feel disrespected.

Let your child know that telling someone these things may scare that person off, at least in the short run. In the long run, however, let her know that an honest exchange, without accusations or name-calling, will probably make that relationship stronger.

OVERCOMING THE FEAR OF REJECTION

What might inhibit a child from reaching out to another in a gesture of friendship? The same thing that might inhibit us as adults: the fear of rejection. One of the differences between children and adults is that we have more experience with rejection. We try not to take it too personally. We understand that some people just don't click. We move on, looking for those who will reciprocate the good feelings we have for them.

We need to explain to our children that rejection is painful and unpleasant, but it is a fact of life. You can say, "It's okay to feel bad after a rejection, but it is not the end of the world." You can also tell your child that it's okay to examine why someone may have rejected her. If she treated that other person poorly, then it's appropriate to determine why she did it and how not to behave that way again. Then decide together if it's worth reapproaching the same person and trying to rectify the situation.

But it's important to make the point that rejection is not something to avoid like the plague. If your child is not getting hurt by rejection sometimes, I'd suggest that she's not out there socializing enough, not taking enough risks, not stretching or challenging herself enough. Let your child know that risk does not always guarantee success. But taking on risks, in this case by attempting to make friends, is a sign of growth and maturity.

As usual, if your child has gone through a rejection, lend a sympathetic ear. Ask how it felt. Ask what she learned. If she responds that she learned not to try to make friends, redirect her to look at how to better pick those with whom to make friends.

Meanwhile, your child may also have to learn the other side of rejection, as the one who rejects. That's not easy either. Your child may have to keep a distance from someone who may be a bad influence, someone who will eventually end up being a bad friend. When he gets older, he may have to say no to someone who loves him but for whom the feelings are not reciprocal. Saying no can sometimes be just as painful as hearing no.

HOW TO LOSE GALLANTLY AND WIN GRACEFULLY

Losing is not easy. But winning can be even harder. Over the years we have been well schooled in the art of losing with dignity. Coaches have taught their players to walk right up to the winners, shake their hands, congratulate them, acknowledge what a good job they've done. We recite the line "It's not whether you win or lose, it's how you play the game." (Have you noticed we quote that line mostly to those who lose?) From a very early age, we tell youngsters who lose—whether it's the game, the election, or acceptance to the college of their choice—to draw some lessons from the experience, to ask themselves what they could have done differently or better the next time. We tell them how much sweeter victory will taste once they have lost at something.

It's all true. And, for the most part, they understand. While they may fear losing *before* they lose, once they have gone through it they realize it's not such a terrible thing.

What we have failed to instruct them well in, however, is winning. To be a good winner—not falsely modest, not overly boastful—requires a certain kind of balance, a self-confidence, a belief that you deserve to win. We may not have prepared our children for winning as well as we've prepared them for losing.

To approach winning with neither embarrassment nor guilt, and (without making the loser feel like a *complete* loser) to truly enjoy the reward of your efforts—these are the finer points of winning that many coaches overlook and that many parents assume their children will know intuitively. They won't learn it from some of their role models, though. Many top athletes, movie stars, rock stars, and supermodels often fail at being winners. They don't show respect for their coaches, their spouses, their fans, or their own possessions. They wreck hotel rooms. They "talk trash." They physically abuse their wives. They abuse their own bodies with drugs and alcohol.

To deal with the stress that comes from winning, you must allow yourself to feel that you *deserve* to win and then conduct the rest of your life as a winner, as a hero others would want to emulate. You must also face the pressure of following your own act, of performing the next time as well as, if not better than, the time you won. The syndrome known as fear of success is predicated on what is expected of you after you succeed. If you help your child understand some of the obligations and expectations that accompany winning—like helping tutor or coach a less successful friend or lending a supportive shoulder to a friend who has lost—you will bring be raising a real winner.

CARING AND SHARING

Children care. The children's KidStress Survey tells us so. Children say they get sad when their grandmother is sick, when

"Dad looks depressed," and when "my brother is going to die." We found that their empathy extends further than we may give them credit for, like when "people hurt others," or when they see "a disabled person, one who is hurt or one who does not have much luck." And then there was the youngster whose capital letters almost screamed from the page: "WILL THE PEOPLE STOP CUTTING DOWN TREES SO THE ANIMALS WILL HAVE SOMEPLACE TO LIVE?"

They also share, even if less often than we'd like. With patience, parents do see that as their children grow their capacity to share also grows. To foster the concept of sharing, parents can do two simple things. Both are variations of the basic ideas I suggest throughout this book.

One is to model. Show your kids how to share by sharing your own things with them, or by calling their attention to times when you share your belongings with your husband, wife, friend, or other family members. If necessary, go out of your way to share something. Bring your child across the street with you when you lend your neighbor a gardening tool. Show your appreciation—verbalize how thankful you are—when someone lends you something. (If you want to be sure this happens, you can set this up by asking your husband or friend in private to ask you if he can borrow something of yours in the presence of your child. And you'd better be prepared to say yes!)

The other way to foster sharing is to reinforce the behavior in your child. Too frequently parents notice only when their children aren't sharing. It's often very loudly brought to your attention when one sibling complains that his brother won't let him play with a toy. When the two are playing quietly together in their room, you may be tempted to take advantage of the momentary peace to do a chore or return a phone call. It would be better to let them know you noticed their cooperation; peek your head into their room and say, "You guys are great, playing together so nicely." Or when your daughter asks if her girlfriend can come over to play, you can respond encouragingly: "Sure, you and Melissa always share your toys so nicely and have such a good time that it would be a pleasure to have her come over." Catch kids being good and they'll go out of their way to do something to have you "catch" them again.

CHAPTER 7

The World—and Everything

Based on what you've read so far, you could argue that children's stress is centered in their own little worlds: their achievement in school, their family, their friends. But children are much more attuned to what is going on in the rest of the world than we give them credit for.

Few parents (10 percent) who responded to the KidStress Survey predicted that their children would say they were stressed by pollution and war concerns. About 40 percent predicted crime would worry their children more. In fact, according to our survey, children worry about safe water and air and nuclear war almost four times more than they worry about crime!

Their concerns run the gamut—from microcosm to macrocosm, from the sublime to the ridiculous, from the here and now to a vast nebulous future they can barely fathom—and sometimes all in the same breath, or the same sentence. Here is a small sample of the things they said they worry about:

"My family, my friends, school, what the world will be like in 2000 and what it will be like in 3000 and beyond that."

"What will happen to the homeless situation or the job situation. Will education get stronger? Did I miss the best day of life? Did I miss out on a real education? Will I be smarter or will my kid sister? Will I ever be a famous singer?"

"Robbers, fires, and carbon monoxide."

"Just about everything lately."

"Report deadlines, tests, war."

"Drugs, death, life in general."

"Not much about my family, but I worry that the world and my school have forgotten their morals and that someday the world is going to be a horrible place."

"Everything."

"Almost everything."

"If I will succeed with my future plans."

"Basically about everything!"

"That we may live forever."

"Just about anything and everything."

"Everything: violence in schools and on the streets, money, moral issues, etc."

"Death, grades."

"Friends, fights, if I'll live to tomorrow."

"About what's going to happen in the next year, and about what's in store for the future of myself."

"Smoking, pollution, the ozone layer, school, and my future."

"School reports, tests, and making something of myself in the world."

"Grades, how others see me, extinction, and pollution."

"I worry about what's going to happen if the world blows up, if my parents die, or if I do too many drugs whether I'll die and stuff."

"Nuclear war, roller coasters breaking."

"Everything you could think of."

"I am usually concerned by just about everything that goes on
     around me."
"How something will turn out once done, and how my parents
     will react to it, also how friends will respond to something
     or someone I am friends with."
"The connection between the people of my family."
"The type of people that my friends will turn out to be."
"What I can do now to survive."
"What future lies ahead."
"The world."

I hear several things going on in these answers. One is that
children's concerns do flip back and forth from intensely personal preoccupations to large global worries. Sometimes it
seems as though they give them equal weight. This may be due
to the fact that many of these concerns have something in
common: children have very little control over any of them.
"How others see me" and "nuclear war" may not appear to have
equal value on a stress scale, but to a child they do. There is a
directly proportional relationship between lack of control and
stress: the greater the sense of loss of control, the higher the
stress. Children can do very little about either nuclear war or
what others think about them. In fact, what I hear in their responses is frustration about how much in their lives—or their
futures—is out of their control. This is understandable.

In re-reading their responses, I also began to hear something
else that gave me a clue about how to help children deal with
the stressors they mentioned. Sometimes, it seemed to me,
their concerns sound almost like a script. It's not that they
don't care, but that many issues they mention do not touch
their lives directly. They are responding to things they have
not experienced themselves, things *reported* to them. Some of
their comments read like headlines, not lessons they're being
taught in schools, not typical family-dinner conversation, not

gossip heard over neighborhood fences or among their own peers. Sometimes they may be parroting concerns they hear their parents voicing, but mostly, I believe, they're repeating what they hear in the media.

KIDS AND THE MEDIA

The problem is not that the media are making children sensitive to big issues; it's that the media are making them too sensitive. There is an overreporting of murders, drugs, and sexuality because these things "sell" news programs to advertisers and viewers. This process distorts both children's and adults' perspectives. Adults have at least the real world into which they go every day to give them some objectivity concerning exactly how much these issues affect their own lives. But how do children, especially at earlier ages, know whether or not every encounter may be disastrous? So children are hit with a double whammy by the media's overexposure of violence, crime, and disaster. Not only are they powerless to do anything about these problems, but they also have no perspective on how severe they are. This generalized fear, in turn, gives them more stress.

A way to help your child begin to gain some perspective involves learning about the various mass media and how they work. Children might not know (and adults need to remind themselves from time to time) that TV and radio stations, newspapers, and magazines are businesses that need to deliver a large audience to their advertisers. In order to garner that large audience, media producers need to air issues they think most people will attend to. You can explain to children that sometimes, in so doing, the media play on people's fears or desires. Kids may come to understand this through the candy-store analogy. TV is like a candy-store window tempting viewers to come in by putting big, sugary, seductive chocolates on display.

With older children, turn on cartoons and point out that the commercials are geared toward young viewers. You can even dissect the cartoons themselves with your children and see how the subject matter is designed to appeal to kids their age. Many kids these days are rather sophisticated; at a rather young age they can grasp how the media work. Just remind them that murder and mayhem may be overreported more for Nielsen ratings than for Columbia journalism awards.

To try to balance the sometimes negative influence of the media, engage your children in a conversation about the positive things they themselves witnessed that were not widely reported in the media. You can also find the bright light in the dark of disaster. When you are watching rescue scenes on TV, help your child find the emergency medical van in the crowd shot, or the tireless rescuers and helpful neighbors. Or comment on the 800 number or address for donations flashed at the end of the piece.

The next thing you can do to help your children deal with worldly stresses is to increase their sense of control by *doing* something on a personal level. Encourage your children to research volunteer groups they could join, organizations they could write to for more information, or local service groups they can visit. Surf the Internet with them for Web sites that will introduce your child to a world of possibilities.

The message should be this: Do something proactive! Recycle, label, sort. Pick up litter. Donate food, old clothes. Join beach and park cleanups. Volunteer at a homeless center. It's your world; take control of it. And show your child that even the small, human-scale things we do make a difference—for others and for ourselves.

Also, monitor your own cynicism and negative comments about the state of the world, politics, or even media coverage.

Be careful of the news you pass along. You may be feeding children's frustration and despair. Remember, parents are the information channel that kids can't turn off.

"THE FUTURE"

When children share their concerns about the future, I hear the same issue again: lack of control. And the younger they are, the more future they lack control of. From their perspective, life ahead—"the future"—looks like a long, daunting journey filled with many potential land mines, detours, and dead ends. So much is expected of them, so much lies ahead, so much is left to go through—years of pop quizzes and exams, of winning and losing, of firsts. There is no handbook to adulthood they can read. Their future must be their teacher.

It's a big world, and they feel like they're being pushed into it. The smallest details can come to stand for the vast implications of the responsibilities they must shoulder in the adult world. I remember when my daughter expressed anxiety about growing up. When we talked about it, she said she was afraid of checkbooks! How did they work? How did you know how much you could spend? Did the bank physically take money out of a vault where all your money was kept? She was focusing all her fear about the responsibilities of adulthood into a checkbook. She was sure she would never figure it out. Of course, she did.

Many kids worry that adulthood happens overnight, like it did for Tom Hanks in *Big*. They worry that they will be equally ill prepared. When a child is asked what they worry about and they say "Everything," I hear a child overwhelmed by fears of the future. He is saying, "I'm stressed about everything I don't understand, everything I can't handle, everything I can't control." When they express fears about their future, couched in various stress symptoms, let them know you and others will be there for them, that for the most part everything they'll need to know will come when it's needed in small, manageable pieces.

One last word about "The future": when we hear children express concern about pollution, disease, and other global issues, I think their real concern is themselves. Behind any voiced concern about the world is a hidden concern about their own future. It comes down to this question: How will all this affect *me?*

The most we can do as parents is to help our children prepare for the future. I don't mean by enrolling them in another set of ballet lessons or speed-reading class. I mean by empowering them with education, positive reinforcement, self-confidence, and tools for living. All of these will go a long way toward helping them deal with their worries about the future.

CHAPTER 8

The Bedtime Blues

For us, as adults, one of life's most comforting and reward-ing moments comes at the very end of an exhausting day, when we slip between warm sheets, stretch our bodies out on a firm mattress, and lay our weary heads on a familiar pillow. Ahhh, sleep, it can be a gentle thing. But sometimes the demons of the day follow you into bed and haunt you all night; balance sheets, responsibilities, and confrontations can fill your dreams, leaving you unrefreshed and stressed-out the next morning.

Almost 50 percent of the children from the KidStress Sur-vey say they also have trouble sleeping when they are under stress. Once again, parents underestimated the situation: only 35 percent of parents who responded to the parents' survey guessed their children have sleeping trouble.

Why do children resist bedtime? The biggest reason is *night-mares,* which top the list of stress symptoms. More than 65 percent of kids taking the KidStress Survey said they have night-

mares once in a while, and another 8 percent said they have
nightmares a lot—close to 75 percent of the children surveyed
said they have nightmares at least sometimes. Parents under-
shot again: 37 percent thought their children ever have nightmares. To a child, a nightmare is like a small shock, and they
fear they'll experience it again the next time they go to bed. No
wonder so many of them have the bedtime blues.

Another reason our kids put up such a fuss when bedtime
rolls around, especially after the nonstop day they've put in,
has to be understood from a child's point of view. If you were
young and every moment of life was offering you yet another
discovery, another explanation, another surprise, another new
and exciting experience to savor, wouldn't you want to stay up
and catch every last second of it? And, as you were getting a little older, beginning to gain a little control over some areas of
your life, beginning to gain control over your own body, learning hand–eye coordination, mastering muscle movement, mastering your bladder, wouldn't you resent someone else telling
you when to go to bed, when you should be tired—while your
own body is telling you that you feel wide awake and ready for
some more excitement?

Once again, parents face a control issue. To children, being
forced to go to sleep when *you* say they should means they've
lost control over one of the most natural phenomena of the human body. And, as we know, a loss of control brings about a
gain in stress. But as we also know (or should), loss of sleep one
night is going to mean more stress the next day. Research has
clearly shown that a deficit of sleep makes the body vulnerable
to illness, due to a decrease in the efficiency of the immune system. So while your youngster may see the bedtime battle as a
clash of wills and a struggle for control, you should see helping
him get enough sleep as one more way in which you can arm
him in the battle against stress.

HOW TO HELP BRING ON THE SANDMAN

First, keep in mind that at the appointed hour, say 8 P.M., you can lead a child to bed, but you can't make him sleep. And don't forget, almost 50 percent of the children surveyed in the poll say they have trouble sleeping when they are under stress. So before you start thinking you've got a child who just wants to defy the bedtime rules, consider what stressful events are happening in his life that may be inhibiting his sleep. While you can't always eliminate the stress, you can at least do things to offset its effect on your child's ability to get a good night's sleep.

The trick is to help your children learn to put themselves to sleep. Exhausting them by roughhousing and letting them run around the house will not work, as it might with an adult. It will pump their bodies with so much energy-boosting adrenaline that they won't be able to go to sleep. It's better to gradually slow them down, to help reduce their heart rate.

- Spend some quiet time with two- to four-year-olds. Sit on the bed. Read to them. Sing to them. Tell them calm, dreamy, relaxing stories with images of warm bathtubs and billowy clouds, not scary tales of monsters and goblins. Rub their backs. Your soothing voice and the feel of your warmth next to them may be just the relaxant they need to feel that they're not going to miss anything and that all is right in their world. Whisper "Good night," and leave the room.
- Make sure they're not getting so much caffeine that it would be impossible for them to sleep even if they wanted to. Look at food labels, and don't forget about the "hidden" sources of caffeine: sodas, hot chocolate, and some candies. Keep in mind that caf-

feine can keep a young person's body stimulated for up to six hours. Make early afternoon the last chance to eat something with caffeine in it.

- Don't waiting too long to put your children down for the night, perhaps in the hope that they'll get really good and tired, may backfire on you. When they are overtired, their bodies will produce stimulating chemicals to fight the fatigue, making falling asleep even more difficult.

- If they say they're just not sleepy—and here sometimes you need to give them the benefit of the doubt—offer them the opportunity to "fool" you. Tell them if they want, they can sit up quietly and look at picture books and fool you into thinking they're asleep. Rather than coming into the living room all evening asking for water or suddenly remembering an important question they need to ask you, they will probably look at books and play in bed until they fall asleep on their own.

- When they're five to eight years old, you can begin to add some *logical consequences* to what happens when they don't go to sleep. I'm not suggesting that you threaten to punish them. Don't even use the word. But you can put your child in charge of her own fate by explaining that each minute she disturbs you after the official bedtime is a minute less you'll be available for playtime or shopping time with her tomorrow. Stay firm, follow through and show you mean it, and very quickly you'll see that this approach works.

- Rewards work also. Not bribes, mind you, as in "If you go to bed now I'll buy you ice cream tomorrow." That will work only so long as you keep delivering the payoff. Besides, you'll be training a sugar junkie.

Instead, wait until your child cooperates voluntarily, *then* offer him verbal praise, support, strokes—and set up some kind of reward system, a chart in his bedroom, for example. For each night he goes to sleep on time, let him stick a star on the chart the next morning. When he has accumulated seven stars— one full week—he gets a privilege. That's called reinforcement—and it works!

Once your kids are older than eight, they will understand the concept of negotiation. Give them options, like a flexible bedtime between 8:00 and 8:30. Let them decide when they want to go to bed, within the times you've laid out. If they start bartering for more time, make that contingent on giving up other things important to them.

If you try to set age-specific limits on your child—saying "You're too young to be staying up this late"—she will hear it as a challenge and want to stay up just to prove to you how grown-up she is.

The morning-after ritual also plays a role in helping your children fall asleep at night. Chronobiologist Scott Campbell suggests you keep their biological clocks on schedule by making sure they wake up the same time every morning, no matter what time they went to bed the night before. Just a few mornings of sleeping in are enough to set a child's sleep patterns off track. The child will be even less tired each successive evening when bedtime rolls around, and the struggles will get increasingly ornery.

Then there are the children whose reluctance to go to bed is due to fear: fear of the dark, fear of monsters in the closet or under the bed, fear of the proverbial things that go bump in the night, fear of creaks and other creepy noises, fear of shadows that look like dragons, fear of having nightmares, fear that they will close their eyes and die in their sleep, or that you will.

Telling your children "There's nothing to be afraid of" won't do the trick. In their imaginative minds, anything and everything is possible. At the younger ages, when they have not yet distinguished between the fantasy of movies and reality, their fears may be based on something they saw on TV or on a video. As they grow older, they read or watch news reports about houses going up in flames in the middle of the night. You need to honor those fears and try to address each logically with your child.

The young boy who insists that his parents stay with him until he falls asleep needs to take more control of his fear. One pediatrician I know suggests that the child fight his imagination with more imagination. If he fears a monster under his bed, help him make a concoction of monster repellant. Mix up water and some gooky stuff and pour it into a water pistol. Let him shoot it under the bed a couple of times. When he wakes up and finds that it worked, he'll feel better (even if he suspects the truth).

Sometimes the solution is as easy as offering a stuffed animal to keep the child company at bedtime. Some parents wonder if a "stuffy" or a security blanket is a good idea or a crutch on which the child will become too dependent. But you can think of such objects as "safe objects." They are not simply crutches but tools children use to build "safe places" in their imagination. Kids have an inborn ability to comfort themselves. Help them use it. Besides, stuffed animals offer comfort simply by being warm and fuzzy. In fact, I know some adults who secretly still cuddle a stuffed animal or stuffed pillow when they go to asleep alone.

CHAPTER 9

Coping with Death and other Scary Facts of Life

Death is a fact of life, one of the most stressful facts of life. When they're not worrying about their own death, many children say they're worrying about the death of a close family member, the death of a pet, or even the deaths of those they don't know whose tragedies are publicized in the media. When kids were asked to name what kinds of things concern them, here were some typical responses:

> "My mother dying and leaving me alone."
> "I worry about what's going to happen if the world blows up and if my parents die."
> "My family dying, tornadoes killing me."
> "Someone dying."
> "A death in the family."
> "If somebody, someday, is going to just go crazy and start firing off nuclear weapons."

In these times, it's no wonder they're concerned—even preoccupied—with death. Even though the majority of children don't witness acts of lethal violence firsthand in their neighborhoods, they probably watch them on the six o'clock news. Or read about them in the newspaper. Teen suicide rates are up. The number of deaths from drug overdoses is still alarming. Your generation probably worried about herpes and gonorrhea; now there's also the deadly acquired immune deficiency syndrome. Death is in the films they pay to see, on the weekly TV cop dramas they watch for free. They hear about it not only in the lyrics of gangsta rap but also in rock, country, hip-hop, and other forms of music.

In real life, a young girl's forty-three-year-old workaholic father, CEO of a Fortune 500 company, dies of a heart attack. A chain-smoking forty-year-old woman dies of lung cancer, leaving behind two sons ages eight and thirteen. A fifty-one-year-old man is suddenly diagnosed with kidney cancer and dies within six months; he leaves a wife and three kids ages seven, twelve, and seventeen. You could tell other stories about the alcoholic whose liver gave out, the sunbather who died of melanoma, the overweight person who just didn't take care of herself and died of multiple complications. All parents.

Meanwhile, perhaps ironically, our children are also seeing people live longer. Their great-grandparents, their grandparents, their parents—and they themselves—have a longer life expectancy than previous generations. This is thanks to modern medicine, plus some adaptations of ancient medicine and a generally more proactive approach to a healthy lifestyle. However, being around older people who are probably in slowly failing health may also make kids think about death.

If you are among the demographic category known as the sandwich generation—raising children and helping support (emotionally or financially) aging parents—there is a double

onus of responsibility on your shoulders when it comes to helping others deal with the stress of death. You've got to try to
encourage your parents to be good role models of aging for their
grandchildren *and* you've got to enlighten your children to the
dignity of approaching death. There are more and more examples of people leading full and productive lives well into their
eighties and nineties. Newspaper, magazine, and television reports feature such people. Show these to both your parents and
your children. In addition, many companies now will retain—
even hire—employees who are beyond the traditional retirement age. Perhaps inviting grandparents to spend more time
with grandchildren—without you around—will inspire them
to appreciate each other more.

DEALING WITH TELEVISED TRAGEDIES

The bottom line is this: people die. It sounds heartless and
cruel, but getting that simple fact across to the children, without morbid drama, is the first step in helping them cope with
loss in their family or in the world.

Their first encounter with death may be through television.
Even if you tried, you could not shield your children from hearing about death if there's a TV on. Network television can, at
any time, interrupt their favorite cartoon show and give a report on a bomb or a hurricane or a police shootout that will jolt
your children into reality.

As I noted in chapter 1, children today see more than thirty
dead bodies a week on the nightly news. They are witness to
countless more deaths in movies. Even cartoons are not without violence: an average of thirty acts of violence appear in cartoons in a given half hour. By age twelve, the average child has
seen more than one hundred thousand hours of violence on
television. When the KidStress Survey asked children about

their biggest health and safety worries, 71 percent of seven- to ten-year-olds said they feared getting shot or stabbed at school or home, and 63 percent worried they might die young.

Call it viewer trauma or vicarious terror, but its effects on children are powerful. Without a context for understanding natural catastrophes like floods or earthquakes, or man-made tragedies like the bombing in Oklahoma City or the murder of O. J. Simpson's ex-wife Nicole Brown and her friend Ronald Goldman, children are left with a feeling that nothing is predictable, that bad things can happen at any time. And when they lose their sense of an orderly world, they lose a sense of control. And that, of course, sets off kidstress. Kids will turn edgy, moody; they may erupt into tears or take out their frustration and anger on their little brother, or their dog.

Seeing the despair and grief of families of victims on the TV news adds to their frustration. "What can we do to help them, Mommy?" they will ask, and you will feel equally powerless. You can't reach out and touch the shoulder of that mourning father on the tube. On top of that, your kids are dealing with their own guilt—"Thank God it didn't happen to our family!"— though they may never even be able to identify it.

We can allay some of our kids' stress, as I said earlier, by assuring them that skilled professionals—emergency rescue squads, police, firefighters, social service groups, and others— are trying to help whenever people are suffering. We can suggest calling a local station or national relief organization to see if we, as a family, can send blankets, canned foods, or money to assist. Maybe we can volunteer at a local center.

Most important, we can talk about it. In all my experience, I have seen again and again that talking out fears, giving them voice, is the best therapy for children and adults. Denial, negation, and apathy will not help. Talk about how bad it must feel. Help your kids put their feelings into words. If they have trouble, ask questions. They will have their own questions. Lots of questions. They will ask the same questions over and over. They are digesting your answers slowly. Each time, answer the questions with patience. Let them know that their feelings are real, normal, and justified.

One other thing to keep in mind: as a demonstration of just how real your kids' feelings are, you should expect the shock effects caused by seeing a tragic news report to last anywhere from several days to several weeks.

Talk about things your own family can do to try to prevent disasters from happening. But be honest about the fact that all the preparation in the world may not be enough. Review with your children important phone numbers of police and fire departments. Show them again where the flashlights and the first-aid kit are.

And, along with your verbal support, give them physical support. Give them the hug you can't give to the people on the TV or in the newspaper. Against the unpredictability of the world, physical affection, arms tightly wrapped around them, is the best way to let them know you love them and will do everything within your power to protect them.

CARTOONS AND AGGRESSION

There's nothing new about cartoon violence. Since cartoons were first created, bunny rabbits have been flattening piglets, road runners have been blasting coyotes to smithereens, and assorted other characters have been pounding each other into oblivion. But the violence in cartoons has been increasing, as I mentioned earlier.

How much is too much violent cartoon watching? It depends on your child. If your child tends toward aggressive behavior, one cartoon with any kind of violence in it may be too much. According to the National Institute of Mental Health, cartoon aggression increases already-aggressive kids' pushy tendencies. For nonaggressive children, the time still may be better spent reading, playing cooperative games, or watching TV shows that promote prosocial behavior.

Some studies have shown that, beyond teaching children to act aggressively, cartoons can teach children other unwanted skills. Just watching those cartoons may pump up kids' adrenaline and desensitize them to screams and pleas for help. They may become accustomed to thinking that the only way to get someone's attention is to rant and rave—like a cartoon character!

So should parents ban Saturday-morning TV watching, one of the all-time favorite activities of children? That would be almost unpatriotic of me to recommend. But I can suggest taking steps to minimize the negative effect of cartoons:

- Give your children an objective perspective. If you watch with them, point out how animation can make things look different from reality. Make sure they know the difference between fact and fiction, especially insofar as human anatomy is concerned. Let them know that real people would not survive if exposed to situations they're watching. Note how special animation effects make things look different than they would be in real life.
- Set time limits. Enough cartoon watching is enough. Let your kids watch, but be firm about when they must stop. (No kid likes to turn off the TV in the middle of a program, so set time limits on the hour and half hour.) Demonstrate your own self-control when it comes to TV. (For example, guys, if you're watching a football game and it's dinner time, get up promptly, turn off the tube, and join civilization.)

- Discuss the cartoons. Try to get your child to verbalize what he may have learned from watching that cartoon. What traits of the "hero" would he emulate? What were despicable? Let him know that the character's angry response might not have been the best way to deal with the situation. Ask your child how she or he might have handled it without breaking something over someone's head. Maybe that character would have gotten what he wanted much sooner by being nice to or patient with the other guy.
- Don't be a cartoon character. If your behavior sometimes resembles a mad and violent character from a bad cartoon, your child is getting the message doubly clear. The aggression she sees at home reinforces that the cartoons may not be so fictional after all, that in real life it's okay to act like Bugs Bunny. But it's not.

SCARY FILMS, VIOLENT TV SHOWS

Some experts say that scary films give children practice at separating fantasy from reality. In so doing, they help them gain control over their own fears. But horror films are not for every child. Not only does each child have his or her own level of tolerance for scary flicks, but those levels can shift at each age and stage of development.

Children two to four years old just aren't developmentally prepared for horror movies like *Scream* or even *Jurassic Park*. They're still dealing with fundamental fears of the dark and sudden noises. Even five- and six-year-olds have such wild imaginations that they are prone to exaggerate things we think of as nonthreatening or obviously fabricated. But somewhere around seven or eight, children become more afraid of being teased by friends for being "scaredy cats" than they are of the movies. So, sweaty palms and all, they'll take on those cemetery scenes.

Because your children all have their own fear threshold, help older children make their own choices. Some can handle animated horror but not live action. Some can handle a video version of a movie on the small screen at home, surrounded by familiar things, but would not feel comfortable seeing it on the big screen in the dark, cavernous, alien environment of a theater. See if you can find reviews of films or get word-of-mouth recommendations from other kids and/or their parents to help your youngsters decide. (Many newspapers now offer brief reviews of films based on their appropriateness for children.)

If you are watching a movie at home with your child, keep an eye on her. Monitor her behavior. If she is barely keeping it together, and you see symptoms of stress (extreme fidgeting, sweating, thumb-sucking, clinging to you), ask her if she wants to turn it off. Let her control the situation. If it's just too much, let your child know there's nothing embarrassing about walking out of the theater or turning off the VCR. Don't tease her. Be sympathetic. Tell her about the time you saw *The Exorcist* when you were all of twenty-five years old and for weeks were afraid to be alone in the house. They'll see that you conquered your fears (or that you had the good sense not to watch any more movies you knew would be too scary).

THE DEATH OF A PET

Children form very strong attachments to their pets. This comes as no surprise, and a true joy, to any parent who has watched his child bond with an animal, whether it's a cockatiel or a cocker spaniel. Kids embrace pets with all their hearts. Through the animal, they learn responsibility, caring, and sharing. They nurse the pet through sickness, they relish the new tricks the pet has learned, and they take great personal pride in the pet's achievements. It's kind of like raising a child in some ways, isn't it?

So why be surprised when kids take the death of a pet very hard? After all, that pet has become a part of the family, sometimes playing the role of sibling substitute or child stand-in. In the KidStress Survey, 72 percent of the children told us they had a pet that died. I was touched by how deeply sad children sounded even when telling us about the death of a pet long after the loss. "I am sad when people ask about my dead dog" or when "I think about my pet J. J. that died a couple of years ago" were among the typical comments we collected.

One reason for the intensity of feeling and the accompanying stress it provokes may be that the pet's death is often the first encounter a child will have with death and mortality, the first experience with this kind of loss and sadness. Be understanding. This is not make-believe. The pet has probably had as much impact on her life as any close relative, if not more. Except for you, there's no one else with whom your child has experienced such reciprocal, unconditional love.

If your child feels responsible for the death of the animal— justifiably or not—he will also be dealing with feelings of guilt. Help him deal with that guilt as you would help anyone let go of guilt. Say: "There's nothing you could have done." "You did all you could do." And repeat over and over: "This was not your fault."

Also, realize that children's reactions will depend on their age and stage of emotional development and maturity. Children under five years old will not understand that the pet has died permanently and may expect it to wake up. From ages five to ten they will get the idea and go through a legitimate grieving period. Expect tears, withdrawal, nightmares, lack of appetite, and upset feelings even at the mention of the pet. (But that's no reason not to let your son or daughter know or express how much the pet was loved and will be missed.) Older children may be similarly moved, but perhaps because they think they're supposed to be too old to mourn the death of a pet, they will withdraw rather than share their true feelings of loss.

One way to help your child grieve is to have a funeral. Let your child organize it: she can make a speech or select lines from poems, she can decide where and when the burial should be, and how to memorialize the spot. She can bury one of the pet's favorite toys with it. After the funeral, a good old-fashioned get together may be in order. Sit around the kitchen table and tell stories about the pet. "Remember the time Taffy barked at himself in the mirror for hours?" On a more serious note, you may want to suggest making a donation in the pet's name to the local humane society.

After the grieving is over, the next question is usually: Should we think about getting another pet? Having suffered the loss once, are the kids (and, be frank, are *you*) going to risk another sorrowful loss? I say yes. The important lesson for your children is that life is full of risks. You can't avoid the potential pleasures of life because of every pitfall they may present. Remind the children of how much you all loved having a dog or cat or whatever. Would they have *not* wanted those good times? But wait until an appropriate amount of time has passed before thinking of getting another pet. In all likelihood, your children will let you know by making the suggestion. Moving too quickly may suggest that your child's pet is replaceable, like a lost hat. You can't replace what has been lost, but life does go on and this is one way to prove it.

A DEATH IN THE FAMILY

I've saved this for last, but it's the one that tops almost every list of stressors: the death of a parent. Though children did not rank it as the thing that most stresses them, its presence is pervasive in their responses in the KidStress Survey. The reasons are so obvious that I don't even need to spell them out. They're all legitimate: aloneness, abandonment, insecurity, distrust, sadness, loss, along with a fundamental questioning of the way the world works, doubts about the future and continuity, a deeper understanding of impermanence. And always the torment of the unanswerable question: Why? Why? Why? Children may feel such a profound loss of control that they walk on wobbly ground the rest of their life.

For a child under seven, a death in the family can be very confusing. Most children in that age range can understand only what they've experienced themselves. They see death as temporary, like sleep, and they expect the deceased to come back any second now.

Children from age seven or a little older up to age eleven usually understand that death is indeed permanent, but they take it very personally. It makes them worry about their own death. While others are grieving about the loss, they may ask many unsettling, self-reflective questions: "Does dying hurt?" "Will I die?" "When are you going to die?"

Since all children, especially teenagers, are egocentric, they may secretly believe that they made the death occur by thinking angry thoughts about the deceased person. Or that the death is their punishment for doing something bad. These children are dealing with not just loss but also guilt. Once again, assure them this death was not their doing.

If a parent dies, the remaining parent will be under double stress—at once mourning a great, great loss and bearing the burden of helping the children through it too. Those children will generally mirror the behavior of the remaining parent.

Funerals offer a chance for a child to draw solace from the whole family. Seeing everyone there together mourning can bring some comfort to a child—as it may for all of those attending. Children will see that it's normal, even healthy, to be sad. And that funerals are not horrible and mysterious, as in some movies. You should prepare them for the fact that some members of the family may express their grief in different ways— some crying endlessly, some silent, others avoiding other people's eyes. Let your child know that he can express sadness in any way he feels is acceptable, and that he should respect other people's way of handling it.

To help your child better prepare for the highly charged emotional setting of a funeral, encourage her to ask any and all questions she has. And try to answer them, no matter how strange you may think they are. Sometimes what kids imagine is far worse than the truth. The important thing is to make sure they feel heard.

So often we as adults are in shock ourselves when there's a death—and if it's your spouse (or even your parent or a sibling) it will be harder still to pay close attention to what the children are going through. If your child starts acting out in ways that demand your attention, you can be sure that she is suffering and needs your warmth. Promote the idea that a funeral is a healing ceremony, a time to honor the life of the deceased perhaps even more than mourn his or her passing.

Again, try to help children feel free to let their emotions out. Some, especially boys, will think the goal is to thwart tears. They don't want to be seen as babies. They may also see grown men crying, and that will frighten and confuse them. Keep reminding them that their feelings and those of everyone present are valid and that no form of emotional expressiveness is unacceptable.

It may take as many as two years for your child to absorb the full impact of a death. Some of the sadness may last a lifetime. But through it all, stay focused with your child on the fact that life does go on. Even when it means that some sadness about the loss goes on too.

kids' Stressors,
kids' Responses

One stress study found that in the course of a typical day we are confronted with some thirty small stress attacks in response to niggling little annoyances. The researchers suggested that the cumulative effect of these bothersome little foul-ups and flare-ups—from spilling the milk to missing the elevator—could be more harmful to our physical and emotional health than one catastrophic calamity.

In their daily lives, children experience these small stressors with much more frequency than their parents realize, my survey shows. The stress takes its toll when young bodies and minds get jolted by these passing moments. Helping our kids learn to deal with stress events as they come up throughout the day, providing them with an approach to stress that becomes a style of living, is the best we can do as parents.

In this chapter I've collected an assortment of things that will stress your child almost daily. I've also assembled a series of behavioral responses to stress that many children will display. You probably could add several of your own to both lists.

What you will read are sensible guidelines, principles more than practicals. Remember Murphy's Law? Anything that can go wrong, will. It should have been called the Parents' Law because it can enable parents to take in stride any problem their children may have. Yet "problem" is the wrong word. Inconvenience, uniqueness, opportunity—any of these are better words to describe stressful situations that arise in the normal course of life.

The operating premise is that your child will not always be picture perfect or fulfill *your* picture of perfection. What fun would that be? Where would the challenge of parenthood come in? Seriously, you can assume that during parenthood you'll have to deal with at least one of the child-size pressures discussed in this chapter. If you and your child haven't tackled one of these by the time your kid is thirteen, you're probably the only ones who can say that.

KIDS' STRESSORS
ATHLETIC COMPETITION

The tremendous popularity of professional sports, the continuing draw of team and even intramural competition from grade school through college (including the growth of women's sports programs), the importance placed on healthy exercise regimes—all have conspired to encourage youngsters to do their best at athletics. But what about the klutz? The kid who gets taunted as "spastic"? The child who isn't a naturally gifted athlete, who has poor hand–eye coordination, or who just doesn't like sports, athletic competition, or physical activities of any sort? She may be the brain in the classroom (which wins points with the teacher) but the bungler on the field (which loses big points among her peers).

Today's world is hard on children who are not athletic. They'll get teased and ridiculed. Being the last one chosen in a pickup softball game can leave some kids with a permanent feeling of being unacceptable.

Parents want to know if they should encourage their children to develop athletic skills or to focus instead on what they are good at. Even before tackling that question, researchers at the Institute for the Study of Youth Sports at Michigan State University suggest that parents should first find out why their child is *not* a jock. Here are some possible explanations:

- The child is not old enough and therefore not physically developed enough to play a certain sport. Tennis, for example, requires a level of wrist strength that may take some kids longer to develop than others.
- The child is not big enough. He may be the right age, but his particular body may not be big enough for that sport. Football is a good example. Kids who are small for their age may end up spending a lot of time on the bench—which never feels good. Sports like swimming or running might be better for smaller athletes.
- The child is not emotionally mature enough. She may not be able to concentrate enough to follow a coach's directions. She may take criticism too hard. Team sports require an understanding of cooperation, the tasks of a specific position on the field, the concept of letting one person be the star scorer and someone else being the key defender.

For the child who may not be a "natural" at sports but who would like to play, however, don't stand in the way. If possible, get him individualized instruction, a private trainer or coach. Emphasize the grace and beauty of the sport. Remind him that he's out there for the sheer enjoyment of it. Talk about "the zone" and other sports analogies that stress the thrill of the game. As part of this, introduce him to sports activities that are noncompetitive. And, at the same time, de-emphasize the winning part. "How you play the game" may be a cliché, but it's a valuable lesson—especially for the child who may have to get used to not winning.

For the child who just doesn't give a hoot about sports, but who gets taunted for her lack of athletic prowess to the point where she is losing sleep or appetite and is visibly upset about it, let her drop out. There are many other things to do: reading, writing, making model airplanes, crafts. But because exercise is important to her health and well-being, work with your child in finding at least one or two enjoyable physical activities that have aerobic benefits, that don't require excellent hand–eye coordination but that will reward her personally nonetheless. Lap swimming is one. Aerobic walks are another. Jumping on a small trampoline if you have a backyard—at first, away from the view of others—might be another choice.

OTHER FORMS OF COMPETITION

The desire to master and achieve is human nature; it's part of our survival instinct. It drives us to crawl quicker, to run faster, to throw farther. In the days of cavepeople, physical achievement could mean the difference between life and death. In modern society, it could make the difference between just getting by or becoming the chair of the board.

We shouldn't thwart the inner drive to master and achieve in children, but as children grow we should help them find socially acceptable ways to foster their competitiveness. We can help them channel that drive into achieving their personal best at whatever they do. And we can help them enjoy the activity for its own sake, whether they win or lose.

In some cases, however, whether they are motivated by their own nature or the role models around them, some kids take mastery and achievement too far. Sometimes well-meaning coaches, parents, or teachers see such athletic potential in a child that they push him or her too hard. Whether they have good intentions to help these children reach lofty goals or selfish intentions to have these children attain dreams they themselves could not, it's a mistake. What my colleagues and I have seen is that these children begin to fear failure more than they enjoy their achievements. They suffer the same kinds of stresses that plague adult workaholics.

Some of the physical warning signs of sports stress include headaches, stomachaches, fatigue, sleeplessness, and irritability—and these symptoms can sometimes be seen in children as young as three. But if you start seeing these signs at any age in a child who is highly competitive, especially in one who doesn't seem to be absolutely thrilled with herself when she *does* do well, slow her down. Keep in mind that she is a child, not a small adult.

Instead of encouraging only head-to-head combat, find ways for your child to participate in unstructured play activities that have nothing to do with winning or losing, too. Remember the old line "All work and no play makes Jack a dull boy." And you can say the same about Jill. Find qualities in your child to praise that are noncompetitive, like his sense of humor or his thoughtfulness. Let him know that the world does not revolve around accomplishments, that people are admired for their interpersonal skills or simply their ability to enjoy the moment, to smell the roses.

Instead of letting your kids feel they need to draw their identity from winning at everything, help them feel powerful in other ways. Ask their advice on projects you're working on, or their opinions about books and films. And let them decide what color their room should be painted or what to make for dinner or where to go for an outing. These are ways they will feel valued just for who they are, not for what record they've broken lately.

And once again, the role you play can make a difference. Demonstrate that it's okay to make mistakes and still feel self-confident. Losing with dignity can be a lofty achievement in itself. So while mastering a backhand or attaining the highest grade in the class is highly commendable—and will look great on their résumé—children still need to learn that they don't have to win at everything they do.

BABY-SITTERS

For parents, the only stress associated with baby-sitting used to be finding one, and at a price that didn't break their budget. Now it's a much scarier scenario. Hearing so much in the news about abductions, physical and sexual abuse, wild parties, or just plain neglect—on top of the slew of movies about scary things that happen when you leave your child alone often with someone you barely know—makes a parent pay much greater attention to the selection and indoctrination of a mature young adult to watch his or her child for a couple of hours.

Our young children certainly hear as much as we do—plus they hear firsthand accounts from their peers, some factual, some highly embellished. So they too have reason to be fearful when the subject of having a baby-sitter comes up.

But before they or we even get to those baby-sitter blues, let's talk about a more fundamental issue that causes stress. It has to do with both you and your child letting go emotionally. As new parents, just the thought of entrusting your child to someone else—even to your parents, who you know brought up at least one child fairly responsibly—evokes anxiety. You form such a bond with your child that you can't imagine him getting along okay without you, and you assume he feels the same way. Your own possessiveness tells you that nobody could care for your child as well as you. Nobody knows his moods. Nobody knows that she loves to have her belly rubbed when she's tired. Meanwhile, your child may be old enough to have similar thoughts ("Only Mommy knows my secret belly-rubbing spot").

Thus, parent and child are dealing with weighty emotional baggage when it comes to baby-sitters. For parents it stems from guilt. You know you really could use some time away from your child, but you think you're a "bad" parent to even feel that way. Children may in turn feel guilty about wanting to get away from their nagging parents, but they also deal with a fear of abandonment.

So with both of you feeling some initial stress about the whole prospect, here are several things to keep in mind to help you and your child cope:

- Bring up the subject early. As soon as your child can understand you, start mentioning the fact that sometimes you'll be leaving her with a baby-sitter. Talk about it as though it were a natural fact of life.
- Find a reliable sitter. Easier said than done, you say? I agree. But ask around among your network of reliable friends whose judgment you trust. Word of mouth is still the best marketing tool for finding a good sitter. Also, place flyers on employee bulletin boards where you work. Place one or check for the same at your place of worship as well. State the qualifications you're looking for: age, experience, restrictions (no smoking, etc.).

- Interview those who respond, and call their references! No exceptions! Tell them you may drop in from time to time when they're sitting—*and do*. Dr. Robert Reiner, a psychologist who specializes in child-care screening, says we tend to spend more time checking out a new car than a new baby-sitter. Give potential sitters a list of responsibilities you'd expect of them. This will let those who work for you know that you take the responsibility seriously, and they will too.

- Involve your child in the decision-making process. Let your child meet the prospective sitter. This is a great litmus test for all parties concerned. You can often tell if two people are going to get along right from the start. You can tell a lot about a person by watching her interact with children, particularly yours. After the rigorous interview, let your and your child's gut feelings be your ultimate guides. Knowing that their desires are influencing the decision—that they have power and control—will help your kids feel comfortable when they finally are alone with the sitter.

DENTAL VISITS

What could be scarier than the thought of a visit to the dentist? Note, however, that the *thought* is frequently much scarier than the actual visit. Despite the fact that dental procedures have become virtually painless, and fluoride has cut down decay, millions of people still would rather do almost anything than go to the dentist. Sadly for children, many of those millions are parents. It's they who probably leave their children with that first association of dentists and fear.

So the first step is letting go of any preconceived notions. The second is to play up the positive side. Promote the idea that going to the dentist is part of a healthy lifestyle. Good dental hygiene will help minimize the possibilities of cavities—and therefore the need for additional dentist appointments. Healthy teeth make you more attractive. And, if you need further artillery, you can suggest that frequent brushing, regular cleanings, and dental checkups will cut down on halitosis!

- Select a kid-friendly dentist. Ask for recommendations—not from your friends but from your friends' children. Some pediatric dentists just have a better way with children. We're not just talking about the ones who give balloons and stickers after an appointment or the ones with the waiting rooms full of toys and puzzles or chairs equipped with music tapes—though that all helps. The critical concern is the dentist's personal style. Is he or she warm and sincere? Does the dentist listen—really listen—to your child when he voices anxieties? Does the dentist have a good sense of humor? If you think it's important or necessary, make an appointment to meet the dentist, with your child of course, so that by the day of the appointment you both don't feel like the professional is a stranger.
- Help your child relax. This may be tough, but the irony is that the more relaxed she is about sitting in the dentist's chair, the less likely she will be to feel any pain. With her body somewhat looser, her muscles won't be clenched up, resisting the dentist every step of the way. Remind your child of the various relaxation techniques that are easily available: deep breathing, listening to soothing music, gentle stretching, tightening and loosening muscles, closing

your eyes and focusing on your favorite quiet space, and so on.

ALLOWANCE ANXIETY

The stress children feel about allowance is directly proportional to how much you turn allowance into a reward and punishment. It was intended as neither. Making it seem that way could lead your child to see the attainment of money or success as a reward or punishment, as opposed to promoting accomplishment for its own sake.

Allowance is an educational tool from which children can learn how to budget money, how much (or how little) it can buy in the marketplace, and how to make critical decisions and choices. That's also why micromanaging your child's allowance will cost him in the long run. You're defeating its purpose. But let him spend it all at the beginning of the week and then have nothing left by Saturday to go to the movies and he'll quickly pick up the concept of budgeting. It may also teach your child how to negotiate for a raise.

Work out with your child what you agree to be an appropriate allowance. Allocating too little will put too much pressure on her; it's too soon to make her start nickel and diming her way through life. Give her too much and she may almost feel pressured to spend it or too guilty if she does spend it. Figuring it out together will force your child to think through how much she spends weekly. It's the first step toward making a budget and managing money. Help kids gain control over money management, and you will save them much stress in adulthood.

TRAVELING ALONE

This subject is not a cause of concern until a child is about five years old, the minimum age most airlines allow children unaccompanied by adults to fly solo. Then it almost immediately becomes of great concern. In these days of scattered and splintered families, of cross-country quickies, of the necessities of juggling work and family as we rush through the second millennium, many young children will be forced to deal with their fears of flying alone. Here's how you can help them:

- Prepare long before takeoff. Long before you ever go to the airport, start preparing your child for the experience. Hopefully you will have flown together so that the youngster knows what to expect from flying. Preview the flying experience. We may take it for granted, but there are strange and scary noises and physical sensations that go with flying. Give him an idea of what to expect, from the wait once he gets on board, to the sound of engines starting, to the possibility of turbulence (like a bump in the road when you're in a car), to when meals are served and movies shown.

- Is the timing right? Judge whether your child is developmentally ready to fly alone. Is she patient, hyperactive, not afraid to converse with strangers? Can she amuse herself alone playing or reading? Does she know when she needs to go to the bathroom?

- How's your separation anxiety? As you know, children follow their parents' lead. If you're nervous about the separation, you can be sure your child will be too. If you're not ready to let her go alone, wait until you feel more comfortable with the concept.

One way to get ready is to try trial separations, increasingly lengthening the time.

■ Do a test run. It always makes a child feel less stressed-out when he knows what is going to happen. So walk him through the procedure. Explain every step of the way—what will happen as you approach the ticket counter, who will be available to him on the plane, who he'll meet when he arrives and exactly where he'll meet them.

■ Focus on the good stuff. Sure, your child will be a little nervous and worried about things that may not go as planned. But keep emphasizing the exciting part. Reinforce the thrill of the adventure, how proud you are that he's taking on this challenge. Talk about the games and wings the flight attendants usually shower on children who fly alone, and the special red-carpet treatment they'll get. And, of course, remind your child that the destination will be well worth the trip.

■ Bring familiar toys aboard. A full carry-on bag can be a comforting friend to a lonely child squeezed in between two traveling execs. Let your child pick the toys, puzzles, books, tapes, and anything else he wants to bring within reason, including a security blanket if necessary.

■ Don't forget that your child is coming home. Remind her that you (and her room, her toys, her friends, her pet iguana) will be right there waiting for her when she comes home. Repeat the phrase "when you come home" several times. Let her know you'll miss her, and tell her what you have planned for her when she comes home. This will give your child a sense of security.

STRANGERS

"Don't talk to strangers." We tell this to our children on the one hand, and then on the other we encourage them to be outgoing, adventurous, and independent. We give them mixed messages. We don't want them to be afraid of people, but we want them to be cautious and discerning. There are enough accounts of kidnappings and other forms of violence that some guidelines are in order:

- Make sure your child understands that most people are not dangerous. In fact, they are kind and helpful and worthy of trust. But explain clearly, matter-of-factly, without high drama or in an alarming voice, that some people are not to be trusted.
- Teach your child to read the clues. Instruct him to look for signs in other people that may reveal whether they are to be trusted: Do they make eye contact? Are they trying to touch you? Do you smell alcohol on their breath? Does their story make sense?
- Go over the basics: Never go in a car with a stranger. Don't unlock the house door to someone who you don't know. Don't accept a gift from a stranger. If anyone touches you in a way that feels wrong or bad, tell him not to. Leave quickly and call for help.
- Rehearse scenarios. "What would you do if . . . ?" Use this quiz game to arm your child with the specifics he'd need in a variety of situations. If he's old enough, make sure he has memorized your phone number or has it in his possession at all times. Make sure he has enough change in his pocket to use a pay

phone (and show him how to use one). Also instruct
him in how to contact the police.

CRITICISM, CONSTRUCTIVE AND OTHERWISE

Nobody likes criticism. But at least by the time you're an adult,
you know yourself well enough to know what you're good at
and what you're not. And you've got enough objectivity and
thick skin to deal with critical comments. For children, it's a
different story. They have little or no idea what they're good at.
Not only that, but it must seem as though every minute of
childhood is spent trying something new, being thrown into
situations that they feel completely insecure about—opening
themselves to criticism and (in their minds) ridicule. Most
of them have very thin skin.

What they desperately want is positive reinforcement. But
they also want someone to show them how to do stuff, hopefully someone who has amnesia and will forget all the clumsy
flubs and mistakes they witness. Unfortunately, that person
does not exist, and some children just won't tackle projects
they think they can't do perfectly the first time, which obviously rules out lots of new opportunities.

As parents, our challenge is to offer our kids guidance in the
form of constructive criticism. But by definition we're going to
have to criticize how they're doing something. We have to encourage them not to get defensive when people try to give
them feedback, especially when there may be a better way to do
something.

- One way to gain their trust is simply to tell them that
  any feedback you give them is meant to help them
  do the best they can. Remind them that you have

their best interests at heart, that you are on their team, in their corner unequivocally supporting them all the way. Regale them with stories of your first flawed attempts at something, hopefully with a punch line about how well you do it now.

■ If you are going to criticize, it's best to start with a positive statement. Commend them for what you see them doing well. Praise them for that accomplishment. Repeat that praise. Make sure they hear about the progress they're making and that what they have achieved is not easy.

■ When you do criticize, offer it in a constructive manner. Not like this: "You're swinging the racket wrong." But like this: "In order to gain more control over where the ball is going, try moving your hand up on the grip a little." Note what they are doing correctly, and reaffirm that it's not that easy—but it is within their reach.

Now, the three "Don'ts":

■ Don't criticize when you're angry, only when you're calm.

■ Don't criticize in public; save it for the privacy of your home.

■ Don't criticize who your children are, just what they *do*. In other words, if they finger-paint on the walls, tell them: "Finger painting on the wall is bad." Not: "You're bad for finger painting on the wall."

■ With regard to *taking* criticism from other people, suggest that your child scan the criticism for useful information about the critic. Maybe a classmate is criticizing your artwork because she wants to be considered the best painter in the class and is jealous or insecure. This is often the case. Also, have your child practice taking criticism without becoming defensive or without countering with criticism of his own. He might practice this line: "Thanks for your thoughts. I'll take them into consideration." Or "Interesting." Period. Here you're asking your child to be a little more mature than the critic. Hopefully, your child will intuitively understand the confidence you have invested in him in that gesture and, in turn, will try to live up to it.

BEING LEFT HOME ALONE

For the estimated two million children under age thirteen who take care of themselves at home after school, the level of stress depends on the child. Their age, maturity, common sense, and basic self-confidence should all come into play in helping you decide how ready or comfortable and able your older child will be to take care of herself for several hours before you come home. In addition, you need to evaluate such factors as how safe your neighborhood is and whether there's some responsible adult close by to whom your child can turn.

But there's also a lot you can do to help prepare children for handling being latchkey kids. Latchkey independence can be a positive and empowering experience for children, a dramatic demonstration that they can overcome stress. One way to help your children be comfortable and confident at home is to prepare them for anything that might come up that would scare them. Give them that "What if . . ." test we mentioned earlier. Ask them:

"What if you smell smoke?"
"What if a fire starts?"

"What if the toilet bowl got clogged and flooded over?"
"What if the phone rings?"
"What if you answer it and a stranger starts asking you
      lots of questions?"
"What if all the lights suddenly go out?"
"What if you get hungry?"
"What if you get really scared?"
"What if a friend calls and wants to come over?"
"What if you hear thunder and lightning?"
"What if you fall and bruise or cut yourself?"
"What if you get a headache or sick to your stomach?"
"What if you get bored?"

Throw in some silly questions too: "What if your favorite TV program is canceled?" "What if a bazillion balloons fall out of the sky?" "What if a clown comes in and gives you all the ice cream you can eat?"

With each question they can't answer, offer a possible answer. Show them where the fuse box is. Write down pertinent phone numbers: yours at work, a close friend or neighbor's, the police and fire departments', and so on. Guide them in putting together their own first-aid kit; include flashlights, Band-Aids, aspirin, and other necessities as well as their favorite candy and a rabbit's foot—or whatever they want that serves as their security object.

Most important, ask them what makes them feel uncomfortable about being left at home alone. If you determine that all the prepping in the world is not going to ease their worries, you may need to come up with alternative day care solutions. But leave open the possibility of their being on their own in the future: "Well, let's talk another time about things that worry you about staying home alone and maybe we can come up with some stuff that will help you feel comfortable with it."

But even if a child seems ready, you may have to anticipate

some of their fears. For example, if they don't like coming home to a dark and silent house—who among us does?—suggest leaving lights and radios on.

Even before you're considering leaving your child alone, you can start preparing her. "Don't touch the stove when you see flames or after it's been on. You'll burn yourself really bad." "Don't let a stranger in the house, because we don't know if this is a good person or bad." Explain consequences without creating a major scare in her.

When you think they're ready, try leaving them alone for half an hour. Build up the periods of time you leave them alone. Teach them to help themselves to cereal or show them where the food is. Something you can do is make sure your home is as safe as possible. Keep very sharp objects out of reach. Is the fire alarm working? Are wires frayed? Are any light bulbs flickering and ready to go out? Is there adequate outside lighting? You'll know the time is right when your child is proud, not scared, of her new responsibility.

HOLIDAY AND VACATION STRESS

We assume that our children see the holidays as a carefree time of endless fun. But consider this: do you? Probably not entirely. There's some anxiety involved. Will the hotel have your reservation? Will the car drive or airplane flight be safe? Will you get along with all the new and old friends, or new and old family you're about to see? Will you be entering unfamiliar surroundings? Will you be able get the Fox News Channel? Will you miss your friends and colleagues? Will the work pile up on your desk?

If these things are stressing you out, you can bet your kids feel the same way, but double! One thing to do is to share your concerns with your children. Together you may be able to allay each other's fears and worries. Again, the best advice is to anticipate what may worry them and together work out ways of coping. Bring pictures of friends if you're going away from home for a long while. Preview new situations. Show them pictures of all the new family (and old) they're going to see if you're going on a family holiday. Share family stories with them; explain the relationships. Have toys and games and books on hand for those boring times.

For children of divorce, vacations and holidays can present their own brand of stress. Divorced parents need to pay special attention during these times. This is not a time to make your child feel like a wishbone that the two adults are trying to split in two. If possible, divide the time equally. Let the child call the other parent—even if it's not your own wish.

Religious holidays are an opportunity to explain the differences between and among the people of the world. They should not be used to create divisiveness. There's enough of that going on anyway.

And make sure that, in all the hustle and bustle of holiday and vacation time, there's downtime—time when you cuddle, time to process it all. Review what you've done and where you've been and where else you're going. Take a vacation from your vacation. Rest. Breathe deep. Exercise. Take naps. Do stretching. Get outside and take a walk. And as much as possible, create little environments that recall home. Try to create some routine or rituals within the chaos of travel or holiday time. Stick to regular bedtime hours. This will relieve some of the stress of change intrinsic in vacations and travel.

WORKING MOMS

Having a job or career is perhaps one of the most common causes of guilt among modern women. Mothers who juggle family and work—whether full- or part-time—worry that the time they spend away from their children is going to trigger harmful short- and long-term stress responses from their kids.

The results of a national study examining this issue should put certain myths to rest. It turns out that the effects of a mother's job on her young children depend mainly on *her* job satisfaction. Sociologists at Ohio State University, interviewing almost six hundred mothers, found that if a mother finds her work challenging, complex, rewarding, and fulfilling to her, she more frequently is energized at work and brings that positive energy—and positive self-identity—home. Her interactions with her children will be similarly positive and up.

However, the study finds that when work is a bore—routine and monotonous, unrewarding and unsatisfying—mothers bring home a negative mood that impacts their children's behavior. Working at such jobs, women will feel distracted and irritable, and that's how they'll act when they get home until they let the effects of work wear off.

What to do? In the best of all possible worlds, you have a highly rewarding job that engages you in a positive way. If you're holding yourself back from advancement because you fear your increased job demands will affect your relationship with your children, this study suggests just the opposite. Even when the work is harder or the pay lower, you'll come home to your children in a much better frame of mind. That positive self-esteem is what your children will pick up on. And isn't that what you want to encourage in them?

If for whatever reason you're currently gritting your teeth at a job that you find substantially less rewarding and challenging than you'd like, try to take a break between work and home so that you can shed some of that stress before you pass it on. Stop off at a gym for a quick workout. Grab a respite at a park, have a few minutes for some tea, read a lightweight magazine (don't review a memo from the boss!), or take a ten-minute walk around the neighborhood before you go into your home.

If you do happen to enjoy your work, don't let yourself get sucked into working overtime too much. Research shows that children (especially boys) of parents who put in routine overtime score lower on school tests than others. That applies to either parent—so, Dads, listen up as well.

Researchers also noticed that mothers who feel extremely guilty for devoting so much time to work they enjoy have a tendency to blame every problem their children have on the fact that they work. Then, in an attempt to compensate for their guilt feelings, too many mothers try to make it up by spoiling and indulging the kids.

Remember that children don't resent you for working. What they resent is that the work takes you away from spending time with them. So forget about sending the kids out to play so you can clean the closet; instead go play with them.

One way to allay your children's anxiety about how much time you spend at work is to show them that "other world" you disappear to so that it doesn't seem so alien to them. Take them to work with you. Introduce them to your co-workers. Show them where you are sitting when they telephone you from home.

Bring them in on a Saturday and let them help you collate papers or perform some other simple task. Or if they're younger set them up on the floor next to you and assign them some "work" while you do yours. For older children it also helps to explain to them your relationship to work: why you do what you do, what value you get out of it personally, how it fits into the larger world. That talk may be a natural springboard for conversations about what they want to do with their lives.

On occasions that you have to be at work, make sure they have all the information they need about your whereabouts and how to get in touch with you as easily as possible.

KIDS' BEHAVIORAL RESPONSES TO STRESS
BED-WETTING

Adults talk about "performance anxiety" in bed. But even earlier, many young children face an anxiety in bed when they find that their young bodies are not yet ready or able to keep them dry through the night. There are many possible causes for bed-wetting—its clinical name is enuresis—but one of them might be the anxiety of doing what they know their parents want them to do before they are developmentally ready.

Bed-wetting is usually a phase and will eventually go away. Generally, the less you make it a problem for your child, the less it will be a problem. However, if the problem persists, consult a pediatrician or child psychologist. If persistent bed-wetting is not addressed, the child may feel it will last forever.

There are many myths that surround this syndrome, but here are the facts:

- Bed-wetting is not a conscious act.
- Often bed-wetting runs in the family.
- Bed-wetters don't sleep more soundly than non-bed-wetters.
- Decreasing fluid intake before bed does not necessarily solve the problem.
- Punishment doesn't help make the problem disappear.
- Bed-wetters come to feel there is something wrong with them if they're constantly reprimanded for it.

Here are some tips to get you and your child through the night (or the morning after):

- Deal with it. When you change the bed, do it without scolding but with the child's help. Change the bed casually, saying, "Next time maybe you can wake up and use the toilet."

- If your child has stayed dry for a while and then suddenly begins wetting his or her bed again, look for some new kind of stress: a move, a new school, divorce, the death of a pet, or even something as seemingly non-anxiety-provoking as moving the furniture around in his bedroom.

- By paying too much attention to bed-wetting, however, you can actually reinforce the behavior. It may be the act that he knows will always draw your attention. It can become his way of saying he is not happy with the way he is being treated about something else entirely.

- If he spends the night at a friend's house, let him bring his own sleeping bag, an extra set of pj's, and a plastic bag for the wet pair. Warn the friend's mother so that she understands the situation and your child doesn't have to explain himself.

- Accent the positive. Tell your child there's nothing wrong with him, that others have the same problem, and he'll outgrow it. Remind your child that you still love him very much and that you want to help him surmount the "inconvenience."

SHYNESS

Sometimes labeling a child as shy is a self-fulfilling prophecy. (The same is true of the "sensitive" label, a category I discuss next.) If a child holds back from people, is slow in making friends, and is quiet and reserved, parents worry that it's because of something they did. More probably it's the child's own temperament. Research indicates that as many as 48 percent of American adults are shy—that is, uneasy in social situations, sometimes to the point where it interferes with their ability to make the most of life.

Most shy kids are truly just born that way. Psychologist Philip Zimbardo and others have suggested it's the sympathetic nervous systems that some kids are born with that predispose them to what we have come to call shyness. Their neural networks seem to be responding to what they perceive as threatening stimuli, and that, in turn, triggers the same hormones that are set off by the fight-or-flight response. This "shy" trait can be measured in infants as young as four months old, says developmental psychologist Jerome Kagan. Subjected to such things as moving mobiles, Q-Tips dipped in alcohol, and a tape recording of a human voice, about 20 percent of the infants display a pattern of extreme nervous-system reactivity. Distressed, they extend their arms and legs spastically, fret, and cry. Most notably, their heart rates soar. These are all indications that these babies' psychological and physiological stress responses have been set in motion. As they grow, these neurally hypersensitive kids learn to avoid situations that might give rise to anxiety and fear.

Dr. Kagan also found a possible link between parents and children that suggest the trait may be largely hereditary. Still another study found that parents and grandparents of inhibited infants are more likely to report being shy as children than the relatives of uninhibited children.

Shyness is neither good nor bad, but may create some problems. We know how much a shy child may be missing out on fun times and interesting people, yet we can sympathize with the anxiety-invoking I-want-to-be-invisible-and-crawl-under-the-nearest-blanket feeling. Our culture makes shyness a negative trait. The United States, after all, calls itself "the home of the brave." For boys and men, the expectations and assumptions about their gender make shyness equivalent to being a sissy. The research shows that while more adolescent girls than adolescent boys are shy, the boys may say it's more painful. However, by the time we all reach adulthood, gender differences in shyness disappear.

Nonetheless, shyness can make a child's development a lot more complicated, certainly affecting his or her self-esteem. It will inhibit her from asking a critical question in school. It will freeze him just as he is about to reach out to befriend a peer. He'll let a bully push him around. She'll squelch a very creative idea for fear it won't be accepted. And maybe worst of all, there will be so many people who will miss the chance to meet that thoughtful and nice person you know your child can be. They won't have the pleasure of meeting your pride and joy!

Are shy kids destined to grow up to be shy adults? Can parents do anything to help shy children steel themselves and be able to walk into challenging social meetings? The answer to both questions is yes. In fact, you can do a lot to help. One is not to be overprotective; if you are, your children will never get any chances to develop the skills they need to find some level of comfort in the world. They will only become more shy and less equipped to deal with people. In fact, one study found that children whose parents do not shield them from stressful situations overcome their own shyness. But it's a delicate balance. If you push children into difficult situations, they will resent you and draw more into their shells.

Though much shyness seems to be hard-wired, remember the role you play too. Shyness can be a style, absorbed by watching others. And who is it they watch from the moment they are born? You.

Some psychological studies also show that shyness may be encouraged when parents are inconsistent in their early-childhood care-giving. If an infant doesn't get a consistent level of tender loving care, an insecure relationship may develop between him and his primary nurturers. The baby brings this insecurity into all his relationships, approaching people tenuously, shyly. Then, as the child grows and people label him as shy, he unconsciously further lives out the label.

To help a shy child there are several things parents can do:

- Don't treat shyness as a flaw in your child's character. Don't ridicule or tease her about it. And in your own mind, don't think of it as a very bad condition that your child has, like a rash you have to get rid of. Given the child's own temperament and any environmental influences, it's sometimes an intelligent defense mechanism, like other attempts to minimize stress.

- Be consistent with your love and support. A shy child can become an insecure child if he feels like he is disappointing his parents. Shower him with unconditional love, respect, understanding, and positive reinforcement. Be especially aware that mixed messages can send a shy child back into retreat.

- Don't shelter your shy child. Remember, children who are afraid of social interaction will never learn the skills necessary to manage their shyness if you allow them to absent themselves from situations they consider difficult. But think about having new playdates at *your* house first, not theirs.

- Don't push your shy child. Forcing children to do things beyond their reach may end up reinforcing the idea that they are not capable of handling such situations. Try to draw your child into win–win situations; for example, introduce her to new kids who you know are upbeat, supportive, and sympathetic.

Domineering children may be a bit much for your kid at this early stage.

■ Be aware that some shyness can be part of an age-stage. Few two- to three-year-olds are outgoing. By six, almost half of all children are still shy sometimes. Shy children (and most all children) will be dealing with additional stress during transitional periods: moving from elementary to middle school or junior high, when they first get braces for their teeth, when their parents are separating, or when the family moves. Be especially understanding during those times.

■ It may get worse during the teen years. With new hormones rushing wildly through their bodies and strange new emotions swirling round their heads, they are going through such dramatic changes that the feelings of I-don't-fit-in consume them. They will feel that much more awkward, that much more self-conscious, that much more shy.

SENSITIVE CHILDREN

Some children grow up being called highly "sensitive," a label like that of shyness. Psychologists classify as many as 10 to 15 percent of all children as very sensitive. They describe these children as:

- Very empathetic and perceptive about people's behavior and emotions.
- More compliant than competitive—almost "too good," according to their parents.
- Intense about everything they do.
- Perfectionists.

The way this translates into behavior is that such children cry easily and get their feelings hurt easily because they're hyperaware of even subtle criticism and teasing. They take everything—sermons, advice, constructive comments, someone glancing at them sideways—personally. All of this, of course, makes them easy targets for other kids, so they get picked on even more than usual.

Dr. Robert Brooks, of the Harvard Medical School, finds that most sensitive children are born that way. Keeping in mind that sensitivity often comes with the gene package included when your child was delivered, consider the following ways to help your child handle it:

- Don't be overprotective. Treat her too differently and you may end up reinforcing the "sensitive" behavior. She'll see herself as different or delicate, and never give herself the chance to change.
- Cope with your child's crying. When a child of ours cries in public, most of us have several responses. One of them is slight embarrassment: Is it disturbing and annoying other people? What does it say about my parenting skills? Will people look at my kid as unhappy? These are all normal worries. Meanwhile, you're also trying to figure out whether and how to discipline your child. You're also wondering what's bugging the kid—is he sick, in pain, hungry?—and the crying's starting to bug you too. Meanwhile, little Joseph is simply upset because the bus driver gave him a mean stare. When your child does cry in public, it's best to just say matter-of-factly that you understand he's unhappy about something and, if it's not an emergency kind of crying, that when you get home you'll figure out how to deal with whatever is

bothering him. And let him know that you would like to help him figure out some way other than crying to make others aware of his feelings and needs. In fact, you can rehearse other forms of communicating distress so that the next time it happens he can use that method instead.

- Practice flubs. One of the things that sends self-conscious, oversensitive children over the stress edge is screwing up in front of other people. Encourage them to realize that we all screw up; it's called the "human factor." Here you can pull out the eraser analogy: if people didn't make mistakes, erasers would have never been invented. You can illustrate how to deal with a flub. Put on a show in the kitchen. Drop something, like a phone book. Then launch into a well-thought-out but modest public apology. Or trip into a room with an appropriate one-liner: "Have a nice trip. See you next fall!" (Hopefully your one-liner will be better.)
- Don't minimize your child's reaction. The goal here is to slowly encourage your child to become a little less hypersensitive. At the same time, you have to honor the fact that his discomfort causes him to feel stress akin to any other real stress. In his experience, the world is being very critical of him. It's real to him, therefore it's real. So show as much sympathy as you can. Try: "I understand this feels terrible for you."

LYING

Lying can be a sign of stress. It can also cause stress. Children think lying will help them avoid stress. If they don't admit to breaking the vase, they reason, they won't face stressful punishment. Instead, they face the stress of being caught in the lie. Hopefully, they begin to realize that the "truth will set them free" before the lie catches up to them.

The *capacity* to lie itself is not necessarily a bad thing. It plays a developmental role. Experts say the ability to lie demonstrates that a person knows right from wrong; otherwise that person wouldn't feel the need to lie. Lying also can show that a person has an active imagination—some kids can think up real doozies. And at times lying is polite, as in the case of social lies that make people feel better about themselves ("Oh, have you lost a couple of pounds, Mrs. Smith?").

Before we start scolding our children for telling a lie, we should try to understand why they did so. As I said, lying can often be an indicator that something else is stressing them. For example, it may reflect insecurity or bouts of low self-esteem. Some children lie to make themselves look better in other people's eyes. They are embarrassed about their poor showing on the math test, so they lie about their grade. They are jealous that someone else's family has more money, so they lie about the house their family has (but doesn't have) in the country. They feel other children aren't paying attention to them, so they fabricate stories about heroic feats they weren't really responsible for.

When you detect these sorts of lies and their motivation, your job should be to let your child know not only that lying won't "fix" the problem, but that he is just fine the way he is. Build up his self-esteem at other times by praising his efforts and offering verbal expressions of positive reinforcement. Keep these other tips in mind too:

- Help your child distinguish between fact and fiction. Young children, especially those with active imaginations, invent stories. Treat them as stories. When they say they have a pony, for example, instead of humiliating them by exposing the untruth, child psychologist Hiam Ginot used to tell parents to say "What a nice story. I bet you wish you had a pony. I too wish you could have one."

- Establish the facts. Sometimes extenuating circumstances explain why your child lied. Or he may be telling a partial truth, in which case you don't want to falsely accuse him of lying.

- Let your child know she won't be harshly punished for breaking the vase: The prime reason for most children's lies is to avoid punishment. But if you can assure your child that "confessing" will not earn her forty days of bread and water she may be more likely to tell the truth.

- Try letting your child prescribe the punishment. Let him be the master of his fate. He will understand the logical consequences of lying if he is the one who comes up with how he should be taught not to lie in the future. Often children's own punishments will be worse than anything you can come up with. And they will take the lesson to heart much more quickly.

- Become a lie detector. Many times you will not get your child to admit to a lie. That's when you have to become a sympathetic Sherlock Holmes. Watch for evasive eyes, mumbling and stuttering, hesitations in answering questions that would ordinarily require no "think" time, exaggerations like "always" and "never," nodding in agreement with himself as he digs himself deeper into the lie. Once you do detect the lie, don't say threateningly, "You're lying!" but give him a chance to "correct" any information he's given you: "Are you sure it happened that way?" Offer evidence that may conflict with his version. The goal is not to "catch" him in a lie but to figure out why he lied and address that cause. Lying is simply a symptom of other things going on.

■ Monitor your own lying. Where do children learn to lie? Once again, it probably starts with you. So if you find yourself lying even about small things, you can be sure your child is picking up messages that it's okay to lie in certain situations. It's just that they're not grown up enough to discern when it's okay and when it's not.

■ Some lies shouldn't be tolerated. Lies at the expense of others should be dealt with as soon as you detect them. Also, if you find that your child is lying about too many things, it may be a sign of greater problems. If you can't help her learn the difference between truth and falsehood, you may want to consult a child psychologist.

IMAGINARY FRIENDS

Parents often worry when they find out their child has an imaginary friend. They shouldn't. Imaginary friends can be one of kids' favorite and most effective stress-coping strategies. Instead of discouraging it, take notes.

Children invent imaginary friends for many reasons. Often it's in response to stress. A child attending a new day-care center may create a menagerie of make-believe play friends to get her through a trying time. An older one may create a friend with whom he carries on a long dialogue to intellectually challenge himself or for company on a long trip alone.

An invisible friend can help a child control impulses he or she knows may not be acceptable. The child will scold the friend for bad behavior, or reprimand him for thinking of taking a cookie.

Yale psychologist Jerome Singer found that imaginary companions are more common among first-born children, probably to help ward off loneliness. He also found that kids who fabricated friends were more imaginative than those who didn't. They also got along better with other children, appeared to be happier, and had a more extensive vocabulary!

Your child may have an imaginary friend you don't even know about. Dr. Singer found that while 55 percent of the parents he interviewed said their child had an imaginary playmate, 65 percent of those parents' children said they had one. Here's what to do if your child has an imaginary friend:

- Don't make a big deal out of it unless your child stops relating to real children and withdraws. You can humor your child, but don't take the imaginary friend away from your child by making it your friend too or by outdoing your child in imaginary conversations.
- Don't be manipulated. When your child refuses to eat spinach because it makes her friend sick, or can't go to the dentist because her friend doesn't want to go, you know you're being manipulated. Your child may use the imaginary friend to test the limits of what can and can't be done. Establish the same rules for the friend that you do for your child.
- Wait and it will go away. Eventually your child will let go of the invisible friend. Often that occurs when real friends enter the picture, or when your child has reached a level of maturity at which he feels he can handle situations alone.

UNDERACHIEVEMENT

"Not working up to his potential." That's what teachers call it. Parents call it frustrating. The kids themselves? They'd just rather be left alone.

As many as one in five American students—many of them bright, intelligent youngsters—fall into the category of under-achievers. They represent all levels of intelligence, but most rank above average to superior, with academic test scores to prove it. They tend to be friendly, obedient kids, rarely disruptive. Their family backgrounds are varied, but most have well-educated parents. And almost 75 percent of them are boys, says psychologist Jerome Bruns, a lecturer at George Mason University and a specialist in a new field examining the phenomenon called "work inhibition."

Are these kids lazy? Unmotivated? Bored? Dr. Bruns describes them as unwilling to try to do their best; they make little if any independent effort. They'll come up with a zillion excuses for not doing their homework. They avoid written classwork and "forget" to do their homework—again and again and again. Teachers get frustrated and angry. Parents start worrying. The kids are miserable; they just want everyone to get off their backs.

What's going on here? It appears that most underachievers from the earliest age tend to be dependent children. Whether it's nature or nurture, they find it hard to become self-sufficient. Their refusal to work alone, their continual putting off of homework, their "forgetfulness" when it comes to homework—all are indirect ways of getting others to step in.

If your child is work-inhibited, you probably find yourself policing, cajoling, threatening, punishing, withholding privileges—all to no avail. Your response is probably only making the problem worse. Your child just wants you to stay with him while he does his homework—and that's exactly what you should not do! It would better for you and your child's teacher to team up and promote more autonomy and independence in your child. Remind him that working alone gives him the freedom to be the boss. His ideas rule! Whatever he says goes when he's working alone. Offer him role models of inventors who came up with their best ideas working alone. Remind him that as soon as he finishes his independent work, he can join his family and friends.

To foster independence, give more support and nurturing to these children than to others. They're probably sensitive to criticism and already feel guilty about underachieving. Your role as a supportive parent is to reinforce their worth to them, remind them of their successes, find small ways they can gain a sense of independence (for example, assign them to complete a very short project or chore to do alone in the basement that is guaranteed to result in a feeling of completion and achievement). Then, give lots of reinforcement.

If you're not sure whether your child fits the bill as an underachiever, ask the school testing and counseling services to check for any neuromuscular or cognitive disabilities, or any other problem (such as attention deficit disorder, about which your child's doctor can tell you more).

Finally, be patient. (By now, if you've been following my advice, you have raised patience to an art form.) You have probably done nothing wrong—unless you've been a doting parent who has conditioned your child to expect, assume, and demand that you be around all the time. In such cases, you should be the last to blame him for being upset when you "desert" him. At the same time that you're trying to be patient, you also have to be firm and clear that homework—and other projects—are his responsibility. You'll help him at *his* request, only. The payoff, you can tell him, is a sense of accomplishment. He doesn't have to share that with anyone. That's also his.

NAIL BITING

The medical term is onychophagia. It can make kids' hands vulnerable to skin infection and can make it hard to handle small objects. Biting down too close to the cuticle can permanently deform children's nails. Not only does the act of biting one's nails look unattractive but it doesn't do much for the looks of one's hands either.

Your child may respond to your requests to not bite his nails by saying "Everyone does it." He is only half right. Half the children who responded to the KidStress Survey said they bite their nails, ranking it fourth among the behavioral symptoms kids reported in the stress survey.

Many kids bite their nails when they are bored or under stress. In both cases they have extra energy and no place to channel it. They're fidgety, can't run around, can't punch anyone. What's left? The good ol' nails. Some children will not stop until they have drawn blood from their fingers. Their fingers constantly bear scabs and hangnails that then catch onto clothing and paper, which causes more pain.

For younger children . . .

- It may be a passing phase. So you may see the habit disappear in a short while. If you tease or scold them, you may make it worse.
- If it persists, try a substitute, like a soft rubber toy they can play with and suck on.
- If they bite when they're bored, every time you see them biting suggest playing with finger puppets, clay, finger-paints, or anything else that will require them to keep their hands busy or covered with gook.
- Keep their nails neatly and smoothly filed. Help

them avoid the temptation by eliminating the need to use their teeth to trim their nails of ragged edges.

For older children . . .

- Chart their habit. Some children may not realize how often they indulge. Over the course of a week-end, work with them to record their nail biting. They can't stop a habit they're not aware of.
- Have them wear gloves in the house. This could work for younger children as well.
- Suggest that they clench their fists. Tell them that every time the urge comes over them, they should squeeze tightly until the urge passes. Pediatricians say it works.
- Try behavior modification. Give out stars or points for every hour or every day they resist biting. Set up a system whereby your child can cash in stars and points in exchange for privileges.
- Try nail polish.

RISKY BEHAVIOR

When singer-turned-congressman Sonny Bono and congress-man Michael Kennedy, son of slain senator Robert Kennedy, both died in skiing accidents New Year's weekend of 1997–98, I was frequently asked if some people actually seek risky behavior.

I believe there are three different reasons why some people do. See if any of them fit your child.

1. It's Inborn. Some people seem to be born with a brain that gets bored quickly and easily. Not necessarily the same as attention deficit/hyperactivity disorder, it can be seen as early as infancy, in babies who repeatedly try to crawl out of their crib, even if it means running the risk of falling on the floor again and again. These babies become toddlers who are into everything. Later they precariously balance themselves on edges of swimming pools or cliffs. At an older age they take more aggressive physical risks. They participate in behavior that borders dangerously on illegal. They also may take highly creative and innovative mental leaps that fall outside traditional bounds of social acceptability. That spirit of risk taking can inspire them to become brilliant intellectuals, courageous soldiers, incredibly graceful athletes or ballerinas—or it can get them into trouble.

2. It's Learned. There are plenty of people around who model risky behavior. When children see people getting away with risky behavior—some even profiting from it—they figure, "It worked for him, it'll work for me." So they try something— anything—off the page. If it works once, they do it again. And again. Until they get bored. And then they move on to something riskier, something that will shoot even more adrenaline through their veins. Then they get known as the daredevil of the family, and the title becomes self-fulfilling prophecy.

Children may also pick up risky behavior from their parents' lifestyle. Others attempt risky behavior to get attention. Even negative attention—like being pulled out of class and sent to the principal's office—is better than "no attention" for some and enough to motivate some children to repeat the behavior.

3. It's a Symptom of Psychopathology. In rarer cases, risky behavior is a symptom of a clinically diagnosable psychological problem, such as depression. But because childhood depression doesn't look like adult depression, parents are less likely to identify it as such. Adults suffering from depression may have trouble getting out of bed; children, however, often throw themselves into activities. What's happening with these young people is that the rush of adrenaline acts like shock therapy or an antidepressant that jolts them out of their lethargy. Older kids may do it with stimulants like cocaine or nicotine. Then they'll bring themselves down with alcohol, a depressant. Younger kids do the same thing with risky behavior. The high-risk endeavor provides the adrenaline high. People get used to, even addicted to, getting their "high-on-life" feeling from dangerous antics. It becomes how they live.

If you think your child may be fighting depression with risky behavior, get professional help.

Whether already programmed into their brains, learned, or the result of a psychological disorder, risky behavior causes stress in a child and, no doubt, everyone close to him or her. One indicator of what can happen to children who don't learn to control such behavior came in a study from Harvard Medical School that found a high ratio between young teens who participate in risky behavior and suicide. I especially took note of a line in the study that included "subtle signs" like refusing to wear a seat belt in the car or a helmet while riding bikes or motorcycles.

Some parents of risk takers wonder if their kids are exhibiting what they term "masochistic" tendencies. In other words, the kids seem to *want* to do themselves harm. Actually, I don't believe that is true. I believe that almost everything a child says and does represents an attempt to make something *better*, to get rid of the uncomfortable effects of stress. In this case, parents need to ask what this risky behavior is a quick fix for. What are they trying to make better? Are they depressed and trying to get an adrenaline jolt? Are they attention deprived? Are they developing physically more slowly than other boys and trying to be the "big shot"? Does she "put out" for boys to prove her feminine appeal? Are they just trying to show their parents that they shouldn't be treated like the family "baby" anymore?

Again, remember that no matter what your child is doing, the intention is probably to take *away* an emotional, mental, or physical pain, not create it. Your job is to try to identify the cause and help your child search for real solutions. Parents of risk takers need to help them discover a personally rewarding and fulfilling channel for their energy. Give up trying to get them to sit still. Instead, help them learn how to use that energy in positive ways.

THE SUGAR-STRESS LINK

You've seen it happen. Give your child a chocolate bar and suddenly she's bouncing off the walls. You're sure the effect of the sugar in the candy is activating her stress response and triggering other negative reactions in her. You assume it may explain her turning from a cooperative Dr. Jekyll into a disobedient Mr. Hyde.

But here's a surprise. Research from Tufts University shows that only a very small percentage of children are actually hypersensitive to sugar. More frequently, the behavior you see may be attributed to a combination of factors: a natural burst of energy, the excitement of having been given a much desired treat, even the suggestibility of parents that the sugar will create such a response. Also, we usually offer candy or other sweets to kids after a meal; that burst of energy could be the result of everything else they ate. Or just their excitement about leaving the table. Even among children who are not sensitive to it, sugar is metabolized very quickly into the blood system and goes to work, then is metabolized quickly and leaves the child with a dip in energy and *cranky*.

Parents who notice their children overreacting to sugar should monitor these other circumstances before deciding their kids are hypersensitive to it. Also, don't use it as a bribe when they start acting out. You may be reinforcing the behavior you're trying to discourage. And control your own candy cravings or you'll be teaching them how to sweeten up their life in the wrong way.

CHAPTER 11

Epilogue

I could conclude this book by telling you what you should have learned by reading it. But what I'll do instead is tell you what *I* learned from doing the research for it and writing it:

- Kids suffer from stress.
- They probably deal with more stress in their young lives than we parents did in ours.
- The things that stress children, and their reactions to that stress, may be surprisingly different from what we parents have thought.
- Parents do not necessarily cause their children's stress; nor can they always "make it go away."
- Children have their own natural stress-coping skills.
- Finally and perhaps most important, there are many ways we can help children tap into those innate skills, reinforce the use of those skills, and guide children toward alternatives to stress-producing behaviors.

In short, we cannot be our children's twenty-four-hour stress reduction and prevention system. Stress is part of life. Rather than trying to shield children from all stress, we'd do better to make sure our children's stresses are "child size." That way, they can begin practicing stress-management strategies (and at an early age) instead of becoming overwhelmed. Practice may not make perfect, but continuing to practice will serve kids well into adulthood.

Besides, I know your children's well-being is vitally important to you. I know this from firsthand experience with my own daughter as well as from my years of working professionally with parents as director of The Stress Program at Mt. Sinai Medical Center in New York City. I know your children's stress stresses you! When you see your child learning to deal more successfully with stress, one of your own greatest stresses will be relieved.

And one last thought. Helping our children learn to cope with stress can be either one of the most deeply rewarding, joyful, and fascinating experiences in life, or it can seem like one of the most frustrating, unnerving, and exhausting experiences in life. So much depends on our perspective. Of course, which perspective we take is entirely up to us. Not surprisingly, I suggest choosing the positive perspective when it comes to stress—one our children will then adopt as well. That would be the goal I hope this book helps you and your children to reach. And along the way to that goal, remember to have some fun with your children.

Happy parenting!

Appendix

These polls, one aimed at parents, the other at children, first appeared on the Prodigy service on July 15, 1997, and remained on-line through August 3, 1997. A total of 724 children under twelve years of age responded to the KidStress Survey, 631 adults to the parents' survey. To make sure those who responded by computer were not an atypical group, both surveys were also given to respondents who couldn't access them via an on-line service. These noncomputer–based polls were called control surveys. Little or no differences were found between the two groups.

Parents should take the parents' survey, answering honestly and then comparing their responses to the children's responses as outlined in this book. It will help you clarify and reexamine your own assumptions and beliefs about children and stress generally—and your children and their stress specifically. To help you understand even better how your kids feel about stress, ask them to take the KidStress Survey, answering just as honestly and "just for fun"! I promise a real eye-opener.

You have my permission to duplicate these polls and pass them along to other children (and their parents). If your child is too young to tackle this alone, you can read the questions aloud and write down his answers for him.

PARENTS' SURVEY

What do you think are the stressors in your child's life? Answer these questions *before* you look at your children's answers. This will help you see the difference between your assumptions and their realities.

1. Would You Say Your Child(ren)—up to Age Twelve—Worry?

_____ A lot
_____ Sometimes
_____ Not often
_____ Not at all
_____ Not sure

2. If You Said "Yes," Do They Worry about Any of the Following? (Check all that apply)

_____ Not doing well at school
_____ Bullies
_____ Being hurt
_____ Having an accident
_____ Getting sick
_____ My parents getting sick
_____ Being punished
_____ Pollution hurting the world
_____ Criminals hurting me

_____ War
_____ Not having enough money
_____ My friends not liking me
_____ My brother or sister telling on me
_____ Kids making fun of me
_____ Having to do something new
_____ Failing at something
_____ Other
_____ Don't worry about anything

3. When They Are Worried or Nervous, Do They Ever Have Any Physical Reactions?

_____ Jumpy
_____ Headaches
_____ Stomachaches
_____ Ready to fight
_____ Sweaty hands
_____ Dry mouth
_____ Nightmares

4. When They Are Worried or Nervous, Do They Do Any of the Following?

_____ Bite their nails
_____ Suck their thumbs
_____ Want to be alone
_____ Fight with their brother or sister
_____ Can't pay attention in school
_____ Have trouble concentrating on homework
_____ Cry easily
_____ Daydream a lot
_____ Feel sick frequently
_____ Have trouble sleeping

5. How Much Say Do They Have about What They Do (Like What Time They Go to Bed, What They Eat, or What They Do during the Day)?

_____ They can choose
_____ They have some say
_____ They don't have much say
_____ They have no say about these things

6. Do You Think They Are Ever Afraid to Tell or Ask You Anything?

_____ All the time
_____ Sometimes
_____ Rarely
_____ Never
_____ Not sure

7. Which of the Following Have They Experienced? (Check all that apply)

_____ Birth of a brother or sister
_____ Moved to a new town or city
_____ Changed schools
_____ Parents separated
_____ Parents divorced
_____ Parent remarried
_____ Family had money troubles
_____ Parent was very ill
_____ Parent died
_____ Pet died

THE KIDSTRESS SURVEY

1. Do You Ever Worry?

_____ A lot
_____ Sometimes
_____ Not often
_____ Not at all
_____ Not sure

2. If You Do Worry, What Kind of Things (about Your Family, Friends, School, the World) Do Concern You?

3. When You Get Worried or Nervous, Do You Ever Have Any Physical Reactions (Like Your Head or Stomach Hurting or Something Else That Bothers You)?

4. Do You Ever Have Nightmares?

_____ A lot
_____ Once in a while
_____ Don't have nightmares

5. How Much Say Do You Have about What You Do (Like What Time You Go to Bed, What You Eat, How You Spend Your Day)?

_____ I can choose
_____ I have some say
_____ I don't have much say
_____ I have no say about these things

6. Are You Ever Afraid to Tell or Ask Your Parents Anything?

_____ All the time
_____ Sometimes
_____ Rarely
_____ Never

7. Do You Do Any of the Following?

_____ Bite your nails
_____ Suck your thumb
_____ Want to be alone
_____ Fight with your brother or sister a lot
_____ Have trouble paying attention in school
_____ Have trouble concentrating on homework
_____ Cry easily
_____ Daydream a lot
_____ Feel sick frequently
_____ Have trouble sleeping

8. Have You Experienced Any of the Following?

_____ Birth of a brother or a sister
_____ Moved to a new town or city
_____ Changed schools
_____ Parents separated
_____ Parents divorced
_____ Parent remarried
_____ Family had money troubles
_____ Parent was very ill
_____ Parent died
_____ Pet died

9. Finish the Following Sentences, If You Can:

_____ I wish I didn't have to . . .
_____ I get angry when . . .
_____ I get scared when . . .
_____ I get sad when . . .
_____ The best part of having a brother or sister is . . .
_____ The worst part of having a brother or sister is . . .
_____ My parents get angry at me when . . .

Index